"'John 3:16 is a beautiful summary of the entire gospel in fewer than thirty words. If the whole Bible had been destroyed or lost except for John 3:16, that would still be enough for any person to come to know God and to receive eternal life,' as Timothy George has noted. Paul Borthwick, a highly respected, well-traveled, seasoned missionary spokesperson, masterfully weaves the meaning of this core mission text with some of his most compelling mission encounters. He brings to life these wonderful words of Jesus in a fresh and practical way."

Marvin J. Newell, staff missiologist with Missio Nexus, editorial director of *Evangelical Missions Quarterly*

"Paul Borthwick skillfully weaves together his missiological expertise—as a global scholar and a crosscultural minister—with a gentle but unignorable call for each of us to live as whole-life, whole-world disciple-making disciples. This invitation comes through sound biblical exegesis and inspiring stories that honor the faithful witness of women and men from around the world."

Ruth Hubbard, vice president, Urbana, InterVarsity Christian Fellowship/USA

"Sometimes, we just need to get back to the basics. And when we do, we often find that we hadn't learned the basics as well as we thought. *Mission 3:16* does this by taking a well-known Bible verse, illustrating it with stories from around the world, and offering winsome applications that make you want to go and do it right away! I have my takeaways already, and if you read this book, you'll get yours."

James Choung, vice president of strategy and innovation with InterVarsity/USA, author of *True Story* and coauthor of *Longing for Revival*

"Paul Borthwick's books have been gifts to the body of Christ and this title is no exception. With great clarity Paul provides a way for people to understand the depth of God's mission and our responsibility within it. I wholeheartedly recommend it to young people wanting to understand how their lives fit within God's greater purposes, and to pastors who want a clear way to help people in their congregations stay focused on what is truly important."

Mary Lederleitner, founder and executive director of Missional Intelligence, author of *Women in God's Mission*

"What do you do when something becomes so familiar that its wonder and magnificence fades into the common and the ordinary? Paul Borthwick's new book takes us into the passion and the heart of the most familiar verse in the Bible, John 3:16. Through extensive study, he examines each phrase of the verse as one would investigate the sides of a prism. Readers gain not only clarity to the history and the call of the words but also discover the urgency of the mission of Jesus' words. This book is for all who are familiar with—or even memorized—John 3:16 and yearn to live a mission 3:16 life."

Sharon Hoover, director of missions at Centreville Presbyterian Church, Virginia, and author of *Mapping Church Missions*

"Paul Borthwick profoundly brings us back to the heart of God's message for us, reframing the familiar and injecting fresh insight into it. It is not only backed by solid exegesis (informing the head) but also by the author's own missional experiences recounted in his uniquely winsome style (touching the heart). Ultimately it is a call to *go* and *do* (engaging the hands). You will never read John 3:16 the same way again!"

Allen Yeh, associate professor of intercultural studies and missiology at Biola University

"John 3:16 is not just some text of Scripture for Paul Borthwick but a life he has embraced and lives out. Ever since we first met in Kasarani (Kenya), I've appreciated his genuine and contagious love for people in God's world in all our diversity. Be it around Boston, where God has brought the world to his doorstep, or other parts of the world he has crisscrossed (including Bela-Bela, South Africa, where we most recently met), Paul both speaks and lives out the love of God in drawing people to his saving grace. I commend *Mission 3:16* to all who have experienced this love of God and are eager to invite others to do the same."

Femi B. Adeleye, director of the Institute for Christian Impact, Ghana

"Paul Borthwick has given us an inspiring and eminently readable introduction to mission. While being steeped in Scripture, the book gives real-life examples of how the principles presented have been applied and also gives practical guidelines on how ordinary Christians can adopt a missional lifestyle. A special value of the book is Borthwick's willingness to grapple sensitively with issues such as lostness, which many today avoid."

Ajith Fernando, teaching director of Youth for Christ, Sri Lanka, author of *Discipling in a Multicultural World*

"C. S. Lewis famously contended that overfamiliarity with a subject can all too easily lead to its unfamiliarity. In *Mission 3:16*, Paul Borthwick successfully helps Christians recover the missional nature of the Bible's most well-known verse. This practical and compelling book is a discipleship resource sure to empower leaders, small groups, and churches all over the world."

Dave Ripper, lead pastor of Crossway Christian Church, Nashua, New Hampshire, and coauthor of *The Fellowship of the Suffering*

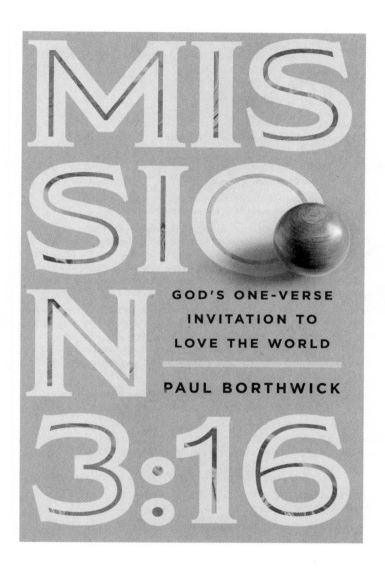

MISSION 3:16

GOD'S ONE-VERSE INVITATION TO LOVE THE WORLD

PAUL BORTHWICK

ivp

An imprint of InterVarsity Press
Downers Grove, Illinois

InterVarsity Press
P.O. Box 1400, Downers Grove, IL 60515-1426
ivpress.com
email@ivpress.com

InterVarsity Press® is the book-publishing division of InterVarsity Christian
Fellowship/USA®, a movement of students and faculty active on campus at
hundreds of universities, colleges, and schools of nursing in the United States
of America, and a member movement of the International Fellowship of
Evangelical Students. For information about local and regional activities,
visit intervarsity.org.

All Scripture quotations, unless otherwise indicated, are taken from The Holy
Bible, New International Version®, NIV®. Copyright © 1973, 1978, 1984, 2011 by
Biblica, Inc.™ Used by permission of Zondervan. All rights reserved worldwide.
www.zondervan.com. The "NIV" and "New International Version" are
trademarks registered in the United States Patent and Trademark Office
by Biblica, Inc.™

While any stories in this book are true, some names and identifying
information may have been changed to protect the privacy of individuals.

Cover design: David Fassett
Interior design: Jeanna Wiggins
Images: recycled paper texture: © Zakharova_Natalia/iStock/
          Getty Images Plus
          abstract paint waves: © oxygen/Moment Collection/Getty Images

ISBN 978-0-8308-4519-4 (print)
ISBN 978-0-8308-3689-5 (digital)

Printed in the United States of America ♾

InterVarsity Press is committed to ecological stewardship and to the
conservation of natural resources in all our operations. This book was printed
using sustainably sourced paper.

Library of Congress Cataloging-in-Publication Data
A catalog record for this book is available from the Library of Congress.

P	22	21	20	19	18	17	16	15	14	13	12	11	10	9	8	7	6	5	4	3	2	1
Y	37	36	35	34	33	32	31	30	29	28	27	26	25	24	23	22	21	20

The greatest human demonstration to me of the unconditional love of God has been my wife of more than forty years, Christie.

I gratefully dedicate this book to her.

CONTENTS

Introduction: *Jesus' Elevator Speech*   1

1   Entering into John 3   7

2   "For God"   17
     God: The Great Pursuer

3   "So Loved"   33
     Love: The Underlying Motive

4   "The World"   43
     The Target of God's Love

5   "That He Gave"   57
     Sacrifice: The Foundation

6   "His One and Only Son"   69
     Jesus: The Center Point of Salvation

7   "That Whoever Believes in Him"   77
     *The Invitation: A Relationship with
     God Through Jesus*

8   "Shall Not Perish"   87
     The Warning: To Escape Condemnation

9   "But Have Eternal Life"   99
     *The Goal: A Living, Vital,
     Eternal Relationship with God*

10   The Challenge   109
     Living a John 3:16 Lifestyle

Epilogue: *Always on Mission*   123

Notes   131

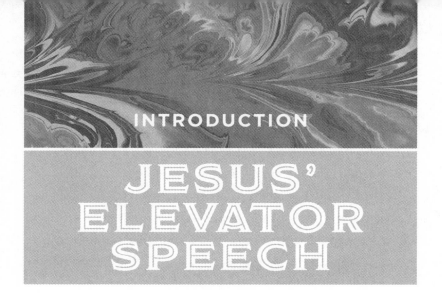

JESUS' ELEVATOR SPEECH

*This is love: not that we loved God, but that he loved us
and sent his Son as an atoning sacrifice for our sins.*

1 JOHN 4:10

G od's mission in the world includes you. Uniquely you. Specifically you. Think through those statements for a moment. God—the Lord of the universe, sovereign over all nations, creator of all humankind, all-powerful, all-knowing, everywhere present—has a mission that includes you! You—created in God's image but rebellious, given the gift of life but still a sinner—are given the invitation to do the mission of God in the world.

For some reason beyond our comprehension, God has decided to do his work through us. Author and missionary Elisabeth Elliot states it beautifully:

Next to the Incarnation, I know of no more staggering and humbling truth than that a sovereign God has ordained my participation. . . . God has arranged things in such a way that His own action is coupled with the action of human beings. The Bible is replete with examples of a loving and powerful God choosing sinful and weak men and women to accomplish His purposes, allowing them the dignity to act in freedom and thus have a *willed* part in what He does.[1]

BUT WHAT IS HIS MISSION?

To be an integral part of God's mission in the world is an overwhelming and glorious thought. But what is this mission? I like simplicity, so I'm drawn to verses or quotations that summarize all of life in a few words. Some examples include the following:

- The commands to "Love the Lord your God with all your heart and with all your soul and with all your mind" and "Love your neighbor as yourself" (Matthew 22:37, 39).

- The question that includes the answers: "What does the LORD your God ask of you but to fear the LORD your God, to walk in obedience to him, to love him, to serve the LORD your God with all your heart and with all your soul" (Deuteronomy 10:12).

■ And the summary of living what God calls a good life:

> He has shown you, O mortal, what is good.
>> And what does the LORD require of you?
> To act justly and to love mercy
>> and to walk humbly with your God. (Micah 6:8)

These and other passages envision a life of obedience as followers of Christ. But they still don't spell out for us God's ultimate mission in the world—the mission that he invites us to join.

JESUS' ELEVATOR SPEECH

When you search the internet for the words "elevator speech," this definition appears: "An elevator pitch, elevator speech, or elevator statement is a short description of an idea, product or company that explains the concept in a way such that any listener can understand it in a short period of time. . . . The goal is simply to convey the overall concept or topic in an exciting way."[2]

If we want a simple, concise understanding of God's global purpose and his mission, and we want a verse with a clear statement of how we join God in his mission, I suggest we turn to John 3:16—the verse that is arguably the most famous, most quoted, and most familiar verse in the Bible. Jesus' ultimate elevator speech is: "For God so loved the world that he gave his one and only Son, that whoever believes in him shall not perish but have eternal life" (John 3:16).

Biblical commentator William Barclay underscores the fame of this verse: "All great men have had their favorite texts; but [John 3:16] has been called 'Everybody's text.' Herein for every simple heart is the very essence of the gospel."[3]

Others describe John 3:16 as "the North Star of the Bible. If you align your life with it, you can find The Way home," "the very foundation of my faith," "the Mount Everest of Scripture passages," and "the Continental Divide of Scripture, the International Date Line of faith . . . the alphabet of grace."[4]

The writers of the *New Bible Commentary* summarize John 3:16 beautifully: God's love is universal, the expression of that love is sacrificial, and the purpose of it is eternal life for believers, who must otherwise perish. They write, "It is no wonder that this verse has been described as 'the gospel in a nutshell.'"[5]

The verse does indeed ring with the awesome sound of being loved by God, the universal song that encompasses the whole world, and the music of salvation through the gift of Christ's sacrificed life. But I sometimes fear that we can rattle off the words from memory without actually dissecting the phrases or contemplating the implications. The verse has had a grand effect throughout Christian history, but what does it mean in our here and now? How does it fit in the concept of God's mission—and our joining in God's mission—in the world? These questions invite our exploration together in the pages ahead.

NEXT STEPS

- Read through John's Gospel chapter three in its entirety.

- Read John 3:16 slowly and out loud. Then commit it to memory in your favorite Bible translation.

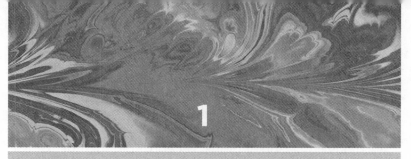

1

ENTERING INTO JOHN 3

*By telling Nicodemus this in such lucid,
simple language Jesus sums up the entire gospel
in one lovely sentence, so rich in content that,
if a man had only these words and nothing of the rest
of the Bible, he could truly by apprehending them
be saved. They flow like milk and honey, says Luther,
"words which are able to make the sad happy, the
dead alive, if only the heart believes them firmly."*

R. C. H. LENSKI

John 3:16 does not appear in isolation. In that respect, it really isn't an elevator speech but rather an amazing summary of the good news of God's love that flows through John's Gospel and the Bible.

The author, John, includes it in a larger story: the account of the religious leader Nicodemus visiting Jesus to ask some questions. John recounts the visit in chapter three, and he starts by explaining that Nicodemus was a religious higher-up—not just an educated member of a group called the Pharisees but also a member of the Jewish ruling council.

Nicodemus comes to Jesus at night, perhaps because he was concerned for his reputation. Jesus was already a controversial figure, especially among the religious establishment. We don't know for certain why Nicodemus came at that time, but it leads to an interesting theory that the nighttime visit provoked Jesus' reference to light versus darkness to describe his life and mission in John 3:19-21.[1]

We do know that the conversation with Jesus made some sort of lasting impact on Nicodemus, who reappears later in John's Gospel when he defends Jesus in front of his fellow Pharisees (John 7:45-52). He also appears after the crucifixion when along with Joseph of Arimathea (identified by John as a secret follower) he comes to anoint and bury Jesus in a decent, unused tomb (John 19:38-42). This association with Joseph of Arimathea implies that Nicodemus was also a secret believer. Perhaps he never left his religious post out of fear of the other leaders.

In their first meeting, Jesus gets right to the point in John 3:7, exhorting Nicodemus to be "born again." The famous nineteenth-century evangelist Dwight L. Moody contrasts the conversation of Jesus with Nicodemus in John 3 with Jesus' conversation with the Samaritan woman in John 4: "It is remarkable that Christ declares the need of an entire change of heart and nature to a man of highest honor, an eminent teacher, and a sincere inquirer; while he speaks the sublime truth 'God is a spirit' to an ignorant and abandoned woman [in] John 4:24."[2]

Moody points out that sometimes the overtheologized or overphilosophized of us need the basic truth of God's love spelled out in the simplest of terms. The brilliant theologian Karl Barth was asked in 1962 during a visit to the United States how he would summarize his essential belief. He replied: "Jesus loves me, this I know, for the Bible tells me so."[3]

Jesus explains *born again* to Nicodemus, and he goes on to introduce him to the pursuing God who desires a relationship with those who have been born again by the work of God's Holy Spirit into the family of God (John 3:3, 5, 7-8). Note that the phrase "born of the Spirit" (John 3:8) indicates that God is the one doing the work; we cannot spiritually "birth" ourselves. Jesus affirms the mysterious work of the Spirit of God in John 3:8 by comparing it to the wind—the impact can be heard, but the source and destination are unknown.

Jesus then describes his own deity as the one who came from heaven (John 3:13) and the one who will be sacrificed (John 3:14-15) so that those who believe will be saved. The reference to Moses lifting up the snake in the wilderness is an allusion to Numbers 21:4-9. While the Israelites were wandering in the wilderness, the people grew impatient with Moses and God and they complained.

As punishment the Lord sent venomous snakes and many people were bitten and died. Moses prays for relief and rescue for the people, and the Lord responds. To provide salvation and healing, the Lord commanded Moses to craft a bronze model of a snake that was placed on a pole. Those who looked up at the snake—the symbol of salvation—lived even if they had been bitten.

The lifted-up symbol of salvation foreshadows the reference Jesus makes here to his death on the cross: when he is lifted up, all who believe in him will be forgiven and saved. In the Gospel of John the phrase "lifted up" refers to Christ's sacrifice three times: here in John 3:14-15, again in John 8:28 (in reference to Jesus' enemies lifting him up), and again in John 12:32 when Jesus claims that when he is "lifted up," he will draw all to himself (see also Isaiah 52:13).

Following on another theme that permeates the Gospel of John, the dialogue of Jesus and Nicodemus refers to believing so as to have life or eternal life. The *Dictionary of Jesus and the Gospels* offers extensive insights into the New Testament use of the words we translate as "life."

> Three different Greek words are used in the Gospels to convey different aspects of the concept of life. *Bios* refers to daily life and one's resources for living. *Psychē* signifies the self-conscious individual self and can often be translated by a personal pronoun. *Zōē* usually denotes life as a gift from God and is often modified by the adjective "eternal" (*aiōnios*). . . .

Zōē occurs thirty-six times in the Gospel of John. In eleven of these occurrences it is the object of the verb "to have" (*echō*) and is used in the context of a promise, invitation or statement about those who believe in Jesus (Jn 3:15, 16, 36; 5:24, 40; 6:40, 47, 53, 54; 10:10; 20:31). . . . In the Fourth Gospel life or eternal life is not limited to a future age but can be realized in the present by the one who believes (*see* Faith) in Jesus. John can still speak of life as future (Jn 5:28-29; 6:27; 12:25), but it is also something that one may possess in the present (Jn 5:24). . . .

The definition of eternal life in John is summed up in Jesus' final prayer: "This is eternal life, that they might know you, the only true God and Jesus Christ whom you have sent" (Jn 17:3).[4]

Bottom line: John is telling us that eternal life—a living and vital relationship with God through Jesus—starts now. This belief and resultant life is the objective of the work of God described in John 3:16. We'll explore this further in chapter nine.

Three other key details help us understand the context of how Nicodemus would have heard Jesus' words. As a Pharisee, Nicodemus lived a spiritual life that focused on avoiding God's condemnation. As a result, Jesus' words about God's love and "believing" so as to avoid condemnation (instead of "doing the right religious things") would have been radical new ideas for Nicodemus (John 3:16-18, summarized by John in 3:36). We'll explore this more in detail in chapter eight.

As a Pharisee and a Jewish religious leader, Nicodemus's world revolved around the Jewish people, Jewish laws, and the restoration of Jerusalem. In light of this worldview, Jesus' reference to God loving "the world" and his use of the word "whoever" would have been shocking if not blasphemous to Nicodemus. The "whoever" of John 3:16, 18, and 21, and later in John 3:33 and 36, is a universal word. The good news of the Gospel is an invitation to everyone, everywhere.

And Jesus' reference to his own deity was a total opposite of Nicodemus's theology. In John 3:16, Jesus describes himself as the "only begotten" (KJV) or "one and only" (NIV) son. The Greek word *monogenēs* literally means "same genes" and could also be translated "unique" or "one of a kind." John uses the same word referring to Jesus in John 1:14 and 18 and again in 1 John 4:9 (an echo of John 3:16): "This is how God showed his love among us: He sent his *one and only* Son into the world that we might live through him" (emphasis added). The phrase "only begotten" from the King James Version indicates that Jesus possesses "every attribute of pure Godhood."[5] Hebrews 1:3 states, "The Son is the radiance of God's glory and the exact representation of his being, sustaining all things by his powerful word."

JOHN 3:16 AS THE MISSION OF GOD

We Jesus followers are called uniquely and specifically to fulfill our part in God's global mission. But to understand our roles, we first need to understand the mission of God into which we are summoned as disciples of Jesus.

I'm suggesting that John 3:16 clearly and succinctly describes that mission. In it, we are introduced to the missionary heart of God: the God who *seeks* after lost people, *sacrifices* to pay the penalty that we deserve, and *sends* us out to carry out his mission in the world.

To summarize the chapters ahead:

"For God": God is the great initiator of mission. He is the starting point, the pursuer of Adam and Eve in the garden. In the person of Jesus, he comes "to seek and to save the lost" (Luke 19:10).

"So Loved": Love is the motivation for mission. God's first message is not condemnation or accusation but love. Unlike most deities of other world religions who provoke fear or demand submission, the pursuing God of Christian faith reaches out to us in love.

"The World": Our entire human population—and even creation—is God's concern. The whole world, all peoples and nations and tribes and languages, is loved by the God who wants everyone to know and respond to that love. The word used for world, *kosmos*, is replaced as "nations" (*ethnē*) in Matthew 28:18-20 and Luke 24:47, but Mark 16:15 refers to "all creatures" or "all creation" (*ktisei*), going past the idea of the human world to all of the living creatures and creation. Tradition indicates that Mark 16:15, "Go into all the world and preach the gospel to all creation," was the trigger for Francis of Assisi's love of creatures and creation.

"That He Gave": Sacrifice is the foundation of God's mission. For salvation to come, God had to give his son as the sacrifice for our sins. And if the good news of salvation and the kingdom of God is going to be spread all over the world, then we, the people of God, will need to make sacrifices—personally, socially, financially, and physically.

"His One and Only Son": Jesus is the pivot around which God's mission revolves. Salvation is found in no one else. Jesus is the mediator, the way, the truth, and the life; no one comes to God but through him (John 14:6 and 1 Timothy 2:5). In our pluralistic world, we want Jesus to be one among many options. But the Bible affirms that Jesus alone is the savior sent by God.

"That Whoever Believes in Him": The mission of God offers an invitation and calls for a response. We understand God's love, receive his forgiveness, and choose to follow.

"Shall Not Perish": God's love blends with his judgment, and as a result condemnation is the consequence of disbelief or rejection of Jesus (John 3:17, 36). God's mission is not just a happy invitation to a relationship with God followed by eternal bliss. It also includes a warning to flee the wrath that is to come—judgment, condemnation, and hell.

"But Have Eternal Life": God's mission is eternally significant for us all. His love, initiative, and sacrifice call us into a relationship with him that will last forever. [6]

We will explore each of these eight components of God's mission and discover where we fit in it.

NEXT STEPS

- Reread John 3, especially the Jesus-Nicodemus dialogue. If you were sitting there with Nicodemus, what questions would you want to ask Jesus?

- Reread the above summary about the upcoming chapters. Which chapter do you look forward to reading most? Which chapter already sounds troublesome?

"FOR GOD"

GOD: THE GREAT PURSUER

> *[John 3:16] tells us that the initiative in all
> salvation lies with God. . . . This text tells us that it
> was with God that it all started. It was God who sent
> his Son, and he sent him because he loved [us].
> At the back of everything is the love of God.*
>
> **WILLIAM BARCLAY**

God pursued me. As a rebellious, church-family seventeen-year-old, I had no intention of following Jesus. My goal as a child of 1970s American culture was "sex, drugs, and rock-and-roll," perhaps with a healthy dose of football and basketball mixed in. I knew the message of salvation, but I reasoned that "when I get old and boring, then I'll trust God."

My parents prayed diligently for their children to come to faith, but I was running the other way. In my junior year of high school, my parents wanted to force me to go to church activities, but I resisted. So they bargained with me. If I wanted to play football (which could mean missing some church—an arrangement that seemed okay with me), they insisted that I go on the youth group winter weekend retreat. The youth group had some nice-looking girls and some winter sports so I agreed, reasoning that I could endure the four or five Bible talks of the weekend.

Much to my surprise, Jesus met me during that weekend. I came away with an overwhelming sense of conviction that I had rejected organized church, but I had never considered a relationship with Jesus. Isaiah 41:10 spoke through my false persona and ego, and the Holy Spirit brought me to himself:

> Do not fear, for I am with you;
> Do not anxiously look about you, for I am your God.
> I will strengthen you, surely I will help you.
> Surely I will uphold you with My righteous right
>   hand. (NASB)

God pursued me. I said yes. And Jesus has defined every aspect of my life for almost fifty years now.

GOD IS THE GREAT PURSUER

For several decades, I taught the Survey of World Religions introductory course at Gordon College near Boston. As any diligent student will know, most of the other great world religions involve human effort toward

God, the divine, or some spiritual goal. Spirituality means increased activity reaching upward—prayers, pilgrimage, sacrifice, and more—so that we can attain divine approval, achieve enlightenment, reach paradise, break the cycle of karma, etc.

In contrast, the God of the Bible comes looking for us, takes on human flesh in the person of Jesus in pursuit of us (see John 1:14), and provides the very avenue for us to come back into a relationship with him.

WHERE ARE YOU?

The biblical account of Adam and Eve in the garden of Eden illustrates God's pursuing heart. Adam and Eve are given a life of fulfillment and beauty, surrounded by perfect creation and in 100 percent relationship with their creator. They are simply told to enjoy everything except for one tree.

The story is familiar: the devil tempts them, they succumb, they eat the forbidden fruit, and they realize that they are naked. Shame and sin enter the world. When they hear God coming, they hide themselves because they sense their naked shame.

God the pursuer comes looking for them. The first words between holy God, creator of all things, and the naked, shame-filled, now sinful people (who God created) is a question: "Where are you?" (Genesis 3:9). Think theologically for a moment: If God knows everything (omniscient), is all powerful (omnipotent), and is present everywhere (omnipresent), why did he ask? He obviously knew where they were, *but he wanted them to know he was looking for them—in spite of their rebellion, rejection, and disobedience.*

Can we grasp the character of God we see here? He came looking—not to judge but to perhaps say, "Where are you? I know you've sinned; I miss you; I want you back." Yes, there will be consequences to their rebellion, but God wants them (and us!) to know that he's looking! In the language of Francis Thompson's poem from a century ago, God is the "Hound of Heaven," lovingly and sometimes sternly pursuing us to bring us back to him.

God's pursuing heart carries through the Old Testament. When the people rebel, God goes after them and restores them. Then they rebel again. But God doesn't give up and ultimately sends Jesus in pursuit of us. Jesus comes as God's incarnational question to all humankind: "Where are you?"

Jesus didn't introduce the idea of reaching out to lost people in the New Testament. He simply came to express in human form God's desire to reach out to lost people. A great example of God's pursuing heart flows through the Gospel of Luke. In this Gospel, Jesus interacts with many that society would reject—the poor, women, lepers, Gentile outsiders, and Samaritan half-breed heretics.

In Luke 15, Jesus tells three parables that express his seeking-after-lost-people heart. After the religious leaders accuse Jesus of "welcoming sinners" and eating with them, Jesus tells the stories of:

- A lost sheep (Luke 15:3-7), where God is the shepherd who leaves ninety-nine sheep behind to look for the one who has wandered away.

- A lost coin (Luke 15:8-10), where God is portrayed as the homeowner who diligently sweeps clean the house looking for her lost coin.

- Two lost sons (Luke 15:11-31), where God is the father who breaks with social convention and runs out to welcome the returning, rebellious son and then again leaves the banquet in pursuit of the older, bitter son.

A few chapters later, Jesus encounters Zacchaeus the tax collector, a despised (and most likely corrupt) member of that society who had sold out his Jewish identity by aligning himself with the Roman government. Jesus goes to Zacchaeus's house, where the people observe disapprovingly that Jesus will be a guest of this sinner. Jesus responds with the seeking-heart mission statement of God: "For the Son of Man came to seek and to save the lost" (Luke 19:10).

GOD'S SEEKING HEART AND OUR LIVES AND MISSION

If we understand that God is the pursuing God, looking for lost people and seeking after people in need of redemption, what does this mean regarding the way we live and join God in his mission?

First, God says, "I pursued you; now join me in pursuing others." "We love because he first loved us" (1 John 4:19), and now we pursue because he first pursued us. If we sense that God came looking for and invited us into a restored relationship with some version of "Where are you?" then we cannot help but want to do the same.

Paul the apostle illustrated this seeking heart when he states to the Roman believers that his ambition was to preach the gospel where Christ was not already known (Romans 15:20). In other words, he wanted to reach out to people in Jesus' name and say to them, "My God wants you back in relationship with him." He aspires to pursue the people who have never heard the good news of the gospel so that they might have the chance to respond. He wants to follow God's example and say to those outside the faith, "Where are you?"

In the commissioning statements from Jesus in both Matthew 28:19 ("Therefore go and make disciples of all nations") and Luke 24:49 ("I am going to send you"), the verb we translate as "go" is in participle form. Instead of the imperative, it should read "as you are going." In other words, he assumes that we are going out into the world in his name, as his ambassadors as stated in 2 Corinthians 5:20, looking for lost people.

Living out John 3:16 means joining God in *his* mission. It means going into each new day with anticipation, what Bob Jacks and Matthew Jacks call "24-7 availability."[1] We go looking for divine appointments: people that the seeking God is preparing to hear the gospel through us!

The fact that God is the source of our mission also reminds us that—in imitation of God—we should be pursuing, seeking, and reaching out to lost people. If God's heart is to pursue lost people and ask, "Where are you?" (Genesis 3:9), and Jesus expresses that mission by stating that he had come "to seek and to save the lost" (Luke 19:10), we need to ask, "Does my life reflect this? Am I reaching out, seeking, and prayerfully pursuing lost people?"

This is not an add-on for the truly committed. This is an integral part of living the Christian life. If fellow Christians constitute the totality of our friendship circle, then we've lost this outward-looking perspective of God.

Second, the God who sends Jesus, now sends us. Related to joining God in saying "Where are you?" to our hurting world, we realize that Jesus now sends us out in the world as his fellow pursuers. In the Gospel of John, God's seeking heart gets expressed by use of the word *sent*. Jesus refers to himself as being *sent* into the world more than forty times. But then, on Easter night after the resurrection, the object of the word gets turned around. Jesus says clearly to his disciples and to us, "As the Father has sent me, I am sending you" (John 20:21).

Here's how this plays out. If we are followers of Jesus Christ, we don't need to ask *if* we are sent. We only need to ask *where* we are sent. God might send us to the ends of the earth, but for now we are sent to the end of the street in our neighborhoods, the end of the hallway in our apartment buildings, and the end of the table in the lunchroom. Scott Sunquist repeats it emphatically in his book *Why Church?*:

- The church, and everyone in the church, is called by God and sent by God.

- We go in [to church] to worship, out to witness.

- Mission means sent.

- All those who are called to Jesus are sent by Jesus.

- Both corporately and individually, the local church sends out its people to be the presence of Christ in the coffee shop, in the dormitory, or at the office.[2]

In spite of being quite bald, I still go regularly to the barber for a trim of the "sidewalls," as I call it. And I choose to go to the barbershop in my town center—not because of their quality or price (though both are good). I choose my barbershop because of Azzeddine and Mohammed, Muslims who came to the Boston area from Morocco. I prepare before going to get my haircut by thinking of a question I want to ask them about their faith, life, or Allah. I pray for them and their families, and I ask God to visit them with dreams, visions, or miracles. Why take my haircut so seriously? Because I am joining God as he pursues Azzeddine and Mohammed through me. I am *sent* to these barbers.

Third, we can be sure that the pursuing God goes ahead of us. The fact that God is the source, the ultimate pursuer, and the sender of our mission reminds us that God goes before us. We join God in what he is already doing. In other words, the pursuing God is the starting point. He has pursued us and we have responded. Now he invites us to join him in pursuing others.

We need to remember that God goes before us, preparing hearts—whether we're in Hamilton or Hungary, Lexington or Lesotho. God is pursuing and preparing:

- That new worker in your office who seems to be following something from the Buddhist faith.

- That fellow you see at the medical clinic who is wearing the beard and turban of the Sikh faith.

- That wealthy secular neighbor with no apparent faith but who might soon be ready to hear the gospel if his financial situation shifts.

- That international student from the People's Republic of China.

THE PURSUING, PREPARING, SENDING GOD

In other writings, I've told the stories of how God goes ahead of us preparing people even as he asks us to join him in pursuing people who are not yet in relationship with him. In *Western Christians in Global Mission*, I relate in detail about a church that committed to pursuing lost people through prayer. They adopted an ethnic specific group in South China called the Miao people, and the church joined regularly to pray, learn, and support efforts to reach out to the Miao. Five years into the meetings, the pursuing God brought a Chinese international student into their midst—an engineering student who had come to the local university—from the Miao people. The church became the physical expression of God's "Where are you?" by offering hospitality to that young man.[3]

God is the great pursuer, but we can be confident because God is going ahead of us. In the work that I do, I've had the privilege of listening to multiple testimonies of God at work to prepare people for the gospel, especially people coming to faith in Jesus from other religious backgrounds. And nowhere is this more evident than in the Muslim world. Consider the following stories.

An international student from Istanbul, Turkey, studying in Boston, was befriended by Christians. Though she was a nominal Muslim, she came to church and enjoyed the community, friendship, and food. But when she was invited to a Bible study to examine the life of Jesus, she declined: "I don't even know my own book [the Qur'an], so I shouldn't study the book" (Muslims sometimes refer to the Christian Bible as "the book" or to Christians as "people of the book"). The Christian friends prayed that she would change her mind. A week later, her mother called from Istanbul and said, "I had a dream; the angel told me to tell you, 'It's okay to study the book.' What does this dream mean?" The daughter told her about the invitation to the Bible study. Her mother responded, "You must say yes. The angel said so." The young woman began a journey that resulted in her eventual decision to follow Jesus. Her mother and sister eventually followed. The pursuing God goes ahead of us—even through angelic dreams.

A man from Marrakesh, Morocco, told me the story of how God pursued him. As a devout Muslim, Ibrahim would go to the mosque daily to pray. He was deeply troubled during his prayers because he kept hearing a voice say: "You won't find me here. You won't find me here." He heard the voice every day and asked his imam (prayer leader), who had no explanation. Ibrahim talked with his brother who then took him to his home and showed him a hidden box. The brother (a nominal Muslim) told him, "Maybe your answer is here" and from the box gave Ibrahim an Arabic Bible that the brother had no interest in but had received when he inquired about a correspondence course. Reading the Bible brought Ibrahim peace. He discovered the correspondence course by Muslim-background Christians in southern Spain. He eventually met them, and they led him to faith in Jesus. The pursuing God goes ahead of us—speaking even at the mosque.

An Iranian (Persian) couple from a Shiite Muslim background now lives in Montreal. I met them at a church I was visiting one Sunday, so I asked them how they had come to faith in Jesus. The young man's story was most dramatic. He had a repeated dream of two hands coming down from heaven, breaking bread. The dream was very intense and so it troubled him, but neither his friends nor the leader at the mosque could explain it. Several years later, he had joined some friends

to go see Mel Gibson's movie *The Passion of the Christ.*
(He explained that many Muslims went to see this movie
because they were told it made Jews look bad.) During
the Last Supper scene, when he saw Jesus break the
bread, the man's dream came flooding back into his
memory. He took the dream to mean that Jesus was
reaching down to him. Through secret contacts with
Christians and many questions later, he was baptized as
a follower of Jesus. The pursuing God speaks out, even
through a Mel Gibson movie!

The pursuing God is at work, going ahead of us even
as he sends us out:

- When the peoples of the world migrate into our
  neighborhoods.

- When the new coworker comes into the office.

- When the resistant relative has a need and asks
  about Jesus.

- When it's time to go to see Azzeddine and Mohammed at the barbershop.

It's an opportunity from God to build a friendship that
can evolve into our being a physical "Where are you?"
from God.

SENT AS AMBASSADORS

"We are therefore Christ's ambassadors, as though God
were making his appeal through us. We implore you on
Christ's behalf: Be reconciled to God" (2 Corinthians 5:20).

After preaching one Sunday morning in the city of Nairobi, Kenya, I departed immediately from the airport for a flight to Addis Ababa, Ethiopia, the next destination on my journey. I was wearing a suit and the two-hour flight was nearly empty, so I appealed to a gracious flight attendant and asked if—given my suit and tie—I could sit in business class.

She smiled at my audacious boldness and granted my request. I sat alone in the business section in my large leather seat. Just before pulling away from the gate, a well-dressed man in a suit took his place next to me. We introduced ourselves, and in the first ten minutes of conversation, I asked the obvious question, "So, what do you do?"

At the question, the man pushed his shoulders back and lifted his head high as if to make a great announcement: "I am an ambassador from Kenya to Ethiopia, and I have been dispatched to deliver a message from our president to the president and government of Ethiopia."

It was clear: his title as an ambassador transformed the way he saw himself. And that of course got me wondering: When Paul the apostle refers to us as ambassadors of Christ, what does that title tell us about ourselves? If we are "sent" (Jesus' words in John's Gospel) as "ambassadors" (Paul's words), how should we see ourselves? Let's examine the roles and responsibilities of global ambassadors.

Ambassadors serve the one who sends them: the president, king, or prime minister. Ambassadors are not independent citizens, but rather selected individuals whose words and actions represent their ruler. William Barclay writes that the word *ambassador* "paints a picture of a man who has a direct commission from the Emperor."[4] In the same way, we are selected and sent to represent our king. We're appointed.

Ambassadors serve in another country. Ambassadors leave their homeland to serve where assigned by the superior. In the same way, we leave the comfort zone of our own spiritual "country" (fellow Christians, the church, our Christian community) to go out into the world to bring the message of our ruler.

Ambassadors deliver the message they're commissioned to bring. Ambassadors who create their own opinions regarding foreign policy or international relations will most likely soon be removed. We've been given the message of good news to bring to the places and people where we've been sent.

Ambassadors serve as a symbolic representative of their nation. At state functions, ambassadors are the physical representative of their nation and ruler. As ambassadors of Christ, people may judge the gospel by the way we represent our Lord.

Ambassadors oversee the process of welcoming people to their country. Ambassadors and embassies determine visa policy and communicate to the host nation how people can get into their nation. We've been given the invitational message of Jesus so that more people can "get in."

Emmanuel Katongole and Chris Rice summarize the word picture of ambassadorship beautifully:

> An ambassador is a representative who bears someone else's message in their absence. Ambassadors live in foreign countries, which they never really call home. Living within a country other than their own, their practices, loyalties, national interests and even their accent appear strange to the citizens of those countries where they are posted. So it is with Christ's ambassadors of reconciliation inside the world's brokenness.[5]

Being an ambassador—sent out by the God who pursues, loves, and scatters us to the whole world—should cause us to throw our shoulders back with a sense of a new identity. We are ambassadors of the King of Kings to the world, with the message of reconciliation through Jesus Christ.

NEXT STEPS

- Review your own story and think through how you've come on this journey of following Jesus. Think through the ways he came looking for you and thank God for pursuing you. Then think of one or a few of the people who were the agents of God—the ambassadors who sought you on his behalf.

- Ask God who in your daily life you can be more intentional about pursuing, befriending, and reaching out to as an ambassador of Jesus.

3

"SO LOVED"

LOVE: THE UNDERLYING MOTIVE

*[John 3:16] tells us that the mainspring of God's
being is love. . . . God is the Father who cannot be
happy until his wandering children have come home.
God does not smash [humanity] into submission;
he yearns over them and woos them into love.*

WILLIAM BARCLAY

Return with me to the classroom and the research into the great religions of the world. In spite of the fact that many devotees of other religions might put us average Christians to shame with the level of their devotion and piety, many (most?) will never talk about a personal, loving, forgiving relationship with Allah, Buddha, Krishna, the Guru Nanak, or their deceased ancestors. They worship, obey, sacrifice, and more, but they often expect no answer from the gods they try to appease or the master to whom they consider themselves slaves. They don't sing songs of intimacy such as "He knows my name" or "Jesus loves me, this I know."

This is not in any way intended to disparage their commitment or their value as people created in the image of God. Instead, I want us who call ourselves Jesus followers to marvel and rejoice that we worship the God of the Bible who acts out of love for us. God pursues us, chooses us, and forgives us because he loves us so much that he sent his one and only son. In our Christian faith and worldview, God loves us, knows our names, watches over us, and keeps count of the hairs on our heads. As followers, we consider ourselves brothers and sisters with the Lord Jesus Christ.

GOD'S MISSION IN THE WORLD IS DRIVEN BY LOVE

As we seek to understand God's mission so that we can understand our own, John 3:16 reminds us that God's first mission is not condemnation. John 3:17-18 remind us of judgment on those who don't believe (we will revisit this in chapter eight), but God's first invitation to belief and relationship flows from love.

Sadly, some of us Christians do not communicate God's love to the world around us. Sometimes we don't want our love for people to get confused with affirmation of their actions, so we come across as negative and condemnatory regarding what we call sinful behaviors.

And in our condemning of the sin, we end up alienating the sinner.

My friend Jack is a wonderful humanitarian (he has spent his legal career defending the human rights of Alzheimer's patients), but he is a self-confessed nonbeliever. When I asked him what he thought of the word *evangelical*, he got quite agitated: "Evangelicals? Those are the people always pointing fingers at others, condemning them and telling them they are wrong or sinners. They're the people that are against everything."

Jack's comments are soberingly sad, especially when we recall that the word *evangelical* is supposed to mean "good news." John Hopler, director of Great Commission Churches, writes, "The word 'evangelical' is associated with something good—that is, 'good news.' It also suggests a vibrant and enthusiastic faith that leads Christians to share this good news with others."[1]

If anything, Christians ought to be the people that exude hope, mercy, and love. We must remember that if love is God's motive, then love should be ours. We pursue because we were pursued; we love because he loves us, as in 1 John 4:9-10: "This is how God showed his love among us: He sent his one and only Son into the world that we might live through him. This is love: not that we loved God, but that he loved us and sent his Son as an atoning sacrifice for our sins."

Think about it this way. How radically would our world be changed if we first viewed other people as loved by God?

LIVING OUT THIS JOHN 3:16 MESSAGE OF LOVE

My seminary professor J. Christy Wilson spent most of his life in Iran and Afghanistan before he came to the classrooms of Gordon-Conwell Theological Seminary in the early 1970s. Of the many lessons he taught us by word and by example, nothing remains stronger in my memory than his example of loving people by lifting them up in prayer. He often challenged us to focus our love prayers toward those who never experienced the love and forgiveness of God through Jesus Christ.

Wilson's challenge to love others by praying connects with the exhortations of Brother Andrew, founder of Open Doors ministry. He challenges every Christian to see the word ISLAM as an acrostic: **I S**incerely **L**ove **A**ll **M**uslims.[2]

We are not called to love Islam; Islam is a religious and cultural system. But we are called to love people, and Muslims are the people in the world of Islam.

I'm always amazed at how many of my American Christian friends have fearful, sometimes hostile, and occasionally hateful attitudes toward Muslims—especially Muslims in our midst. Have they ever taken a course on understanding and responding to Islam? No. And when I ask if they have ever talked to or befriended a Muslim, they answer no. Rather than forming their views of these people through the filter of love, they focus on the actions of a few extremists, listen to the most hostile news reporting, and cross the street to avoid meeting a Muslim in their midst.

After the terrorist bombings at the Boston Marathon in April 2013, people in the Boston area were very nervous about the Muslims in our communities. I was traveling from Boston's Logan airport about two weeks after the bombing. As I stood at the gate waiting for my flight, I noticed a young woman standing very much alone at her newspaper stand. She wore the hijab head covering of a conservative Muslim woman. I sensed that the Lord wanted me to speak to her. I approached her and greeted her with "As-salaam alaikum," the Arabic greeting that means "Peace be unto you." The woman burst into tears.

I immediately thought I had insulted her, or said something wrong, or pronounced a word incorrectly. I apologized and asked what I said wrong. She said, "No, what you said was perfect. I'm crying because I've been standing here over two weeks now since the Boston Marathon bombing, and you are the first person who has even spoken a word to me."

Her name was Aisha. I remembered Professor Wilson and breathed a prayer for her. But I also remembered Brother Andrew and wondered, "How will someone like Aisha ever know God's love if everyone in our community avoids her?"

LIVING OUT JOHN 3:16 WITH A LIFE OF LOVE

God's mission is motivated by love—even love toward people who do not respond or reciprocate. Romans 5:8 describes God's action of love: "God demonstrates his own love for us in this: While we were still sinners, Christ died for us." Note especially that God's love is demonstrated, not just announced, and that God's love is given to people who don't deserve it. The life of love—imitating and reflecting the sacrificial love that God has already demonstrated toward us—can take on many forms.

For Bill Henson and his team at Lead Them Home (leadthemhome.org), it means advocating for a Christian worldview of love toward those in the LGBTQ community, a community that our Christian community often rejects. For Dave and Trish and their church in a resort community, it means putting their convictions into action by helping economically challenged families (many led by single moms) by providing meals to food insecure children (capekidmeals.org). Both organizations serve as a demonstration of God's love.

Look for churches motivated by the love of Jesus, and you find Christians standing for the rights of desperate immigrants, hurting refugees, abandoned children, physically handicapped people, and more. My friend Jack's comments about "evangelicals" might be true of the finger-pointers who often get the controversial news coverage, but if he looked deeper he could find Christian communities that are genuinely trying to demonstrate the love of God.

On a global scale, I see Christians who live in places where Christianity is a small percentage of the population in a country dominated by another religious worldview or political system that's hostile to Christianity. These brave believers look for ways to serve as agents of reconciliation in our broken world and to live a life of loving forgiveness. They demonstrate God's love in their willingness to forgive their persecutors. These men and women understand that we live under the sign of the cross, so they see both the sacrifice of our Lord and his grace in forgiving his persecutors.

God's abiding love enabled Gladys Staines to forgive the religious extremists in Odisha (formerly Orissa), India, who brutally burned to death her husband and two young sons in 1999.[3] It is that same grace that enabled Lalani Jayasingh to forgive (and later serve) the religious extremists who shot and killed her husband in southern Sri Lanka.[4] It is the love of God that enabled Nairy Ohanian to go back to serve in Turkey in a community that persecuted her Armenian grandparents.[5] And love is the motivation for perseverance in the life of Libby Little, who has kept serving the people of Afghanistan even after her husband was killed there in 2010.[6]

GOD'S LOVE CHALLENGES THE SPIRIT OF JONAH

Ask a child coming out of a Sunday school lesson why Jonah ran away from God's command to go and preach to the people of Nineveh, and they might respond by stating that Jonah was afraid of the Ninevites. After all, these Ninevites (part of the powerful, expansionist, violent Assyrian empire) were famous for their atrocities and hostilities toward those they conquered. Jonah knew that, as did everyone in the Middle East at that time.

So out of fear, Jonah ran. Right? Read all four chapters of Jonah and we discover something else.

Jonah was called east but ran west, caused a storm to surround his escape boat, got thrown overboard, lived inside a great fish for three days, and was regurgitated on land. God calls again and Jonah finally relents, repents, and goes to preach in Nineveh. Amazingly, a revival comes. The people of that great city are spared, and Jonah is furious. He sits and sulks, hoping for fire to drop from heaven and melt the city and its inhabitants.

Jonah 4 tells us it wasn't fear of the Ninevites that caused Jonah to run the other way toward Tarshish. He feared God's mercy toward the people he hated and wanted destroyed. "He prayed to the LORD, 'Isn't this what I said, LORD, when I was still at home? That is what I tried to forestall by fleeing to Tarshish. I knew that you are a gracious and compassionate God, slow to anger and abounding in love, a God who relents from sending calamity. Now, LORD, take away my life, for it is better for me to die than to live'" (Jonah 4:2-3).

The love of God demonstrated through the life, death, and resurrection of Jesus Christ means that he might call us to demonstrate love to people we'd rather avoid, at the least, or condemn, at the most. But realizing that this love was demonstrated toward us while we were still sinners means that we are called now to demonstrate love toward others—even the "Ninevites" in our lives.

NEXT STEPS

- Think of one or two people who are regularly but perhaps superficially in your life every week or several days a week. Try to come up with one or two ways that you might demonstrate love toward them the next time you see them.

- Over the next week, go to operationworld.org or https://joshuaproject.net and learn about an unreached people group who you can start loving through your prayers.

- In your quiet moments, ask the Holy Spirit to reveal any person or people that are your Ninevites, people you'd rather see God reject than love. Ask the Spirit to help you to see them the way God does.

4

"THE WORLD"

THE TARGET OF GOD'S LOVE

[John 3:16] tells us of the width of the love of God.
It was the world that God so loved. It was not a nation;
it was not the good people; it was not only the people
who loved him; it was the world. The unlovable and the
unlovely, the lonely who have no one else to love them,
the [person] who loves God and another who never
thinks of him, the [person] who rests in the love
of God and the rebel who spurns it—all are
included in this vast inclusive love of God.

WILLIAM BARCLAY

When I first made my commitment to follow Jesus, pastors or youth workers taught us to change the wording of John 3:16 and insert our names rather than "the world." So my personal John 3:16 went like this:

"For God so loved *Paul Borthwick* that he sent his one and only Son . . ."

I presume that this paraphrase intended to affirm my individual self-esteem and to make God's love more personal, but it also fueled a dangerous individualism that is present throughout much of our Western culture's interpretation of Christianity. We can sing "Jesus loves *me*, this I know" without ever having to come to grips with the thought that Jesus loves that other guy, that other nationality, that other political party person, that other ethnically different person.

While I can indeed affirm that Jesus loves me, and I can celebrate that I am part of the love of God expressed in John 3:16, I diminish the challenge of the global, crosscultural, multiethnic world that Jesus is telling us God loves.

GOD'S MISSION IS TO INVITE EVERYONE

Go back to the actual setting of John 3, the dialogue between the religious leader Nicodemus and the rabbi Jesus. Both men sat there with their great Jewish heritage and with significant knowledge of most of what we now call the Old Testament.

As Jesus talked, Nicodemus wondered about the matter of being born again by the Spirit in John 3:9. He probably hesitated at the reference in John 3:14 about Jesus being "lifted up." But up to this point in the conversation, he was most likely in full agreement with what Jesus was saying. Nicodemus knew about the pursuing, initiating God who came looking for the people of Israel again and again. He could remember the words of Deuteronomy 7:7-8 where the Lord tells the people of Israel that they were chosen—not for their size or impressive power—because God had "set his affection" on them and "loved" them.

In John 3:16, Jesus comes to the target of God's love. Nicodemus most likely expected Jesus to say, "God so loved the Jews," or "God so loved the people of Israel," or the "Hebrews," or "the Chosen." But Jesus told Nicodemus, "God so loved *the world*"!

How did Nicodemus respond? Did he object? Did he sit up straight in startled disagreement? For the Pharisee Nicodemus, God's love for "the world" was probably far beyond his Jewish-centric worldview. He most likely had a very ethnic-specific perspective on salvation and God. God's chosen people were the Jews, and the God of Abraham, Isaac, and Jacob was *their God*. God's long-term pursuit was to bring back the tribes of Israel. God's love was focused on Nicodemus's religious and ethnic kin.

But Jesus' words, "God so loved *the world*" might have awakened Nicodemus to the Old Testament passages that he had conveniently forgotten or selectively deleted. Perhaps Jesus' words awakened Nicodemus to God's blessing to Abraham, his call to the Israelites to fulfill his mission, or the passages from the psalms citing God's concern for "the nations" or "all the earth." I wonder, did Jesus' reference to God's love for *the world* remind Nicodemus of the following facts?

■ God promised to make Abraham great and, through his prodigy, *"all peoples on earth* will be blessed" (Genesis 12:3, emphasis added; see also Psalm 67 for the same "blessed to be a blessing to the nations" theme).

■ God used Joseph to save the nation of Egypt—the nation that God would use in turn to save the family of Israel.

■ The Messianic promise in Psalm 2:8 included a promise to give the Messiah the nations as an inheritance.

■ The psalmist urged the worshipers of Israel to "declare his glory among the nations, his marvelous deeds among all peoples" (Psalm 96:3).

■ Though looking after those already in the family of God was important to God, he said it was "too small a thing" (Isaiah 49:6) to care only for Israel and their restoration. In that Isaiah passage, God reminds the people of Israel of his mission for them—to be a "light for the Gentiles, / that my salvation may reach *to the ends of the earth*" (emphasis added).

As Nicodemus listened to Jesus, I imagine that he was confronted with the biblical truth that the global mission of God was always that the "ends of the earth" would be invited into the family of God. What the Israelites had seen as a privileged calling that gave them special access to God was actually not something just for them. Instead God wanted them to hear his global commission to declare his glory to the nations, the ends of the earth, the world, and all creation. Evangelist Dwight L. Moody summarized it this way:

God's first covenant had been—

(1) With a person, in Abraham [Genesis 12:1-3].

(2) Then with a family, in Jacob [Genesis 28:14].

(3) Then with a nation, in the people of Israel at Sinai [Exodus 19-34]; and

(4) Finally, with "the world," embracing all the other three, in Christ [John 3:16].[1]

LOOK EVERYWHERE

Jesus' message to Nicodemus and the John 3:16 message for us is that no one should be left out. Every person should have an opportunity to respond to God's invitation for salvation.

The phrase "God so loved *the world*" should serve as a sobering reminder to us that there are literally billions of people in our world who have not heard the invitation to respond to God's love and then enter into a personal relationship with Jesus. In other words, these folks have no family member, near neighbor, local church, or Bible in their own language from which they can learn about Jesus. There might not be a radio broadcast or printed materials that describe God's love and the sacrifice of Jesus to pay for our sins and offer us forgiveness. They know nothing of Jesus' resurrection,

Holy Spirit power, or living in daily fellowship with the God who created everything.

To drive this point home, the leadership team at one church decided to insert the reality into their Sunday morning communion service. In their usual church tradition, the servers passed out the bread and the congregation held it until the pastor spoke a rhetorical question: "Has everyone been served?" The question was followed by the phrase: "Then take and eat: the body of Christ given for you." Then the servers would pass out the cup, representing the shed blood of Jesus for our sins. The same question from the pastor was followed by: "Take and drink."

One Sunday, the pastor and outreach leadership team coordinated communion together. They wanted to drive home the point about people who have still never heard about Jesus. When the bread had been distributed, the pastor asked, "Has everyone been served?" Rather than sit in silence, people in international attire across the sanctuary stood up and spoke, one by one: "I represent the Uyghur people of western China, and we have not yet been served." "I represent the Tubu people of northern Niger, and we have not yet been served." "I represent the Karakalpak people of Kazakhstan, and we have not yet been served." Others stood and identified people groups considered unreached or unengaged. (Unreached people might have Christian workers in their midst, but they do not yet have a self-reproducing Christian community. Unengaged people have no Christians working in their midst.[2])

The pastor paused and then reflected, "As we take of this communion bread today, let us remember that there are billions of people and thousands of people groups who do not yet know anything of Jesus' sacrifice, resurrection, and forgiveness that we celebrate today."

After more people groups were introduced, the pastor closed the service with these words: "Let us go into this week remembering and praying for the peoples of our world who will not know of the love and invitation of God unless someone crosses a culture, learns the language, and lives with them as a messenger."[3]

LIVING OUT JOHN 3:16

If the thought that God so loves the world and wants everyone to be invited to the gift of believing and thus eternal life seems a little overwhelming to you, you are not alone. With more than seven and one-half billion souls on planet Earth, none of us can love "the world." Instead, we can look for starting points.

A few years ago during the Christmas season, I stared at one of those tabletop manger scenes and observed the three wise men with their camels presenting their gifts. Putting aside the biblical errors in the scene (see Matthew 2:1-16), I got to thinking about those magi and where they were from. A little research revealed that they were most likely from the area we know as modern day Iraq or Iran. This lesson resulted in a conversation with a man from Iran, and I told him how special his people were to God. He asked me why I would say such a thing. I explained that people from his part of the world were among the first to see *Isa Al-Masih* ("Jesus the Messiah" as it appears in the Qur'an). The Qur'an teaches that Jesus was born in Bethlehem. I wanted him to know that the phrase "God so loved *the world*" included him!

Thoughts of loving the "world" might be overwhelming, but we can all do something to expand our global impact. Todd Johnson, global statistics expert and coeditor of the *Atlas of Global Christianity*, writes:

> Migration is increasing religious and ethnic diversity around the world. 200 million people are on the move today, carrying with them their cultural and religious backgrounds. At least 720 million have now settled permanently outside of their culture's main country. Almost half of these are Christians, representing about 16% of all Christians. There are also Muslims, Hindus, and Buddhists living in large numbers outside of their homelands.[4]

Johnson also points out that never have so many people been on the move, and never have they been so unwelcome![5]

With these mass migrations of peoples, we may have the opportunity to reach people that were up to this point considered unreached, because now they are all around us. The world is changing before our eyes. In Toronto, one of the most international cities in North America, Dr. John Hull, who was then serving as pastor of

The Peoples Church, told me, "God called us to go to all nations. We didn't go, so he's bringing all nations to us!"

We can get involved and informed through global networks such as the Lausanne Movement, where the emphasis is "connecting influencers and ideas for global mission" (lausanne.org), or the World Evangelical Alliance, which works to connect church movements together in more than 125 nations (worldea.org).

We can expand our global prayers for the people of other faiths that we find in our midst, and start relationships with international students at our local universities or new citizens who have come from places where the gospel is not known.

And my favorite way to get involved is simply getting your household together to learn about and pray for the countries on the labels of your clothes. Check out the "made in" label, find the country, look it up on operation world.org for facts and ways to pray, and pray! God loves the Muslim, Hindu, Buddhist, or other person who made your clothes.

WHAT DO YOU THINK I BELIEVE?

Over the last few years—at least in my country, the United States—the word *evangelical* has been thrown around so much that many Christ-following people have grown afraid to use it.

At its core, it's a good term. The word derives from *evangel* or "good news," and John 3:16 is often the theme verse of anyone associated with the term. The good news is the message of John 3:16. An *evangelical* is a person who (according to John 3:3) has been "born again" by believing the message of John 3:16. *Evangelism* is sharing the message of John 3:16. And *evangelistic* describes those committed to the declaration of the *evangel* in word and deed.

But times have changed. A cadre of Christian leaders gather together to wrestle with whether or not we should still use the term.[6] Churches with the word *Evangelical* in their church name or their denomination grow wary and choose more neutral words.

Living in the Boston area all of my life, I've grown accustomed to being a part of a misunderstood, sometimes maligned, and often separate community identified as *evangelical*, but I've decided to take a different approach. Rather than trying to replace the word or even redeem it, I've chosen to make it a word to stir conversation.

I do a lot of flying, and my evangelistic background training always has me looking for opportunities for conversation with seatmates. When a conversation gets going, there comes a point of self-identification (usually in response to the "So what do *you* do?" question). In the past I've self-identified as a teacher, youth worker, consultant, and more. But more recently, my response has been, "Actually, I'm an *evangelical* minister."

The immediate response has been fascinating. A Harvard University professor looked at me and exclaimed,

"I have never met one of you," as if I were some sort of alien visitor. A few seatmates cut the conversation short and went back to their reading. But most of the time, before a person can respond, I insert the question, "Now that I've identified myself as an evangelical, what do *you* think I believe?"

The conversation after this question goes in all sorts of directions. A few people my age or older have asked if I was in the same belief camp as Billy Graham. Others have asked if I was part of the group that burns down abortion clinics. One fellow asked (humorously, I think), "Are you packing heat?" It was clear that he was asking if I was carrying a weapon because, for him, *evangelicals* are associated with the National Rifle Association. Sadly, his theory might be partly true. A few who call themselves evangelical seem to defend the Second Amendment (the right to bear arms) and oppose gun control more than they defend the sixth commandment ("You shall not murder," Exodus 20:13).

If I ask someone what they think *evangelical* means, I need to brace myself for all sorts of questions—often provoked by the way that some politicians or the news media use the term. When asked, "Are all evangelicals white, Republican, middle-class voters?" I explain that my wife and I are registered Independent and that many evangelical African American and Latino Christians vote Democratic. When asked, "Why does it seem like evangelicals' only ethical and moral priority is the unborn, but they stay somehow silent about care for refugees or those needing social assistance?" I try, in a gracious, self-critical way, to distinguish between being pro-life (which would include protecting the God-created value of the unborn, the poor, the immigrant, the refugee) versus simply being pro-embryo (where the objective focuses primarily on bringing the unborn to term). I've even tied my pro-life convictions to our commitment to be concerned as Christians for global environmental issues, because all of our lives are tied to our physical life on this earth.

But the best result of taking on the challenge of the word *evangelical*? More than half of the time, the conversation develops into one of two questions: either, "So what exactly does the term *evangelical* mean?" or "So why do you call yourself *evangelical*?" And from that question, I either share my own story of coming into a relationship with God through Jesus, or I simply unpack John 3:16 as the most concise expression of God's good news.

NEXT STEPS

Think of the world in your midst (your community, fellow workers, international students, and people you meet that are from another country, culture, or religion). Choose one or two of the ways listed below to increase your knowledge of the world that God loves and sends us into.

- Take a course, attend a seminar, investigate a website, or read a book on understanding the beliefs of other religions.

- Learn more about the other countries of the world, keeping in mind that the population of North America is only about 7 percent of the world, according to the United Nations.

- Attend something related to learning about other cultures—festivals, a wedding, food tasting, etc.

- Learn about one of the unreached people groups on joshuaproject.net and adopt them, either by yourself, with your household, or with your Christian community.

5

"THAT HE GAVE"

SACRIFICE: THE FOUNDATION

This is how we know what love is: Jesus Christ
laid down his life for us. And we ought to lay
down our lives for our brothers and sisters.

1 JOHN 3:16

I had the privilege of attending the Third Lausanne Congress on World Evangelization in Cape Town, South Africa, in October 2010.[1] Of the many amazing people I met and presentations I observed, five stood out. All of these involved some type of suffering related to the gospel.

An eighteen-year-old woman from North Korea testified about the loss of her father, but she proclaimed through her tears that her passionate dream was to return to North Korea to share the good news of Jesus Christ.

A bishop in the Anglican church of Nigeria who serves in the Middle Belt area, where Christianity and Islam are most in conflict, testified about he and his wife staying faithful in their ministry even after his wife was attacked by religious extremists. Every husband in the audience gasped as he spoke of these attackers doing "unspeakable things" to his wife. And yet they have persevered.

Libby, a missionary veteran of more than two decades of service in Afghanistan, testified about God's faithfulness after her ophthalmologist husband and his team were murdered while working in rural Afghanistan. Yet she was faithfully pushing forward.

The entire arena of four thousand participants lifted in the air over two hundred chairs to symbolize the Chinese participants who were forbidden by their government from coming to the conference, after they had raised all their support internally.

Beyond these stories, I remember meeting Farshid. One evening after the meetings had ended, I was having coffee with a friend when I met David, a leader in Elam, a ministry dedicated to the training of pastors in Iran.[2] I asked David if there were any Iranian pastors at the conference. I had never met an Iranian believer, much less a pastor!

David introduced me and my colleague to Farshid. We were transfixed by his story as he radiated enthusiasm for Jesus. He had become a follower of Jesus Christ out of his Shiite Islamic heritage, and after training, he was now involved in church planting with multiple new congregations made up of Muslim-background believers.

I came home inspired by Farshid's testimony and his courage to lead in a place where opposition to the gospel is blatant. I committed myself to pray for him. Over two months after the Cape Town congress ended, I received word from a friend at Elam that Farshid had been arrested and sentenced to six years in Rajai Shahr, one of Iran's worst prisons. His sentence later became seven years. He lost his health, he released his family to exile (for their safety), but he didn't lose his faith. Though severely persecuted and tested, Farshid was finally released early in December 2015.

His story and these testimonies all serve to remind us that sacrifice comes with the territory of following Jesus on his mission in the world. We follow the Lord who laid down his life as a servant for us (Philippians 2:5-11), so we shouldn't be surprised when we read about the suffering of others or when we are called to suffer ourselves.

God's mission of pursuit, love, and global reach is built on the foundation of suffering. And all that we do is built on our response to the sacrifice Jesus made for us. In imitation of that, we join in sacrificial giving of our lives and resources—though few of us will ever suffer in the way that Jesus did. Nevertheless, 1 John 3:17-18 urges us to take the sacrificial example of Jesus and implement it in the way we respond to those in need.

THE CHURCH IN MISSION INSPIRES US TO SACRIFICE

In the affluent, middle-class life many of us live—at least in North America—I often think that we have replaced the biblical Trinity with our own trinity: comfort, convenience, and consumerism. When asked to serve across cultures, we ask first, "Is it safe?" long before we ask if God is calling us to go as our part in his mission. We fear giving up our lifestyles of over-choice, our oversized cars and houses, and our dreams of health and wealth. The prosperity preacher Joel Osteen observes that we want our best life now![3]

But if we look at both the current state and the history of our global Christian family, we cannot avoid being inspired to join in making greater sacrifices—financially, socially, and even with our security. Consider the following examples.

An inspiring mission movement coming out of China (which I cannot name here due to security reasons) aspires to send Christian workers across the Buddhist, Hindu, and Muslim worlds. They estimate that 10 percent of their sent ones will be martyred.

British star athlete of the late nineteenth century C. T. Studd gave up his lucrative sporting career to serve in Africa, India, and China. His motto was, "If Christ be God and died for me, no sacrifice I make is too great."[4]

I've had the privilege of attending student "mobilization for mission" conferences through a variety of networks, including the International Fellowship of Evangelical

Students and the World Evangelical Alliance. In countries such as Uganda, Nepal, Ethiopia, China, and Cuba, I've noted the older leaders organizing or sponsoring these conferences. Many of these older Christians spent time in prison for the faith, suffering greatly under Idi Amin in Uganda, Hindu nationalism in Nepal, Mengistu Haile Mariam in Ethiopia, Chinese communism, and the oppression of Fidel Castro's government in Cuba.

At a student mission conference in Accra, Ghana, more than four hundred university students came together to give their lives by taking the gospel message in word and deed to the ends of the earth, especially to the tough places where Jesus had never been preached. The first four speakers—all Ghanaians—told stories about the British missionaries who first brought the gospel to Ghana in the mid-nineteenth century. They reminded the students that their faith was a result of people coming to Ghana who literally died while bringing the gospel message to the students' Ghanaian forefathers and foremothers. As young adults, the British missionaries set sail from England, having packed their earthly belongings in their own caskets because they knew that they would most likely never return home from West Africa. An estimated 60 percent of these servants of Christ died in their first two years of service. In one location, a graveyard bears the headstones of the children of missionaries who died as their parents served: most of those children were younger than ten years old.[5]

The stories of sacrifice characterize life for many in other parts of the world where Christianity faces fierce opposition. On a visit to one of my friends who teaches in Beijing, China, I attended a church with four young men who were new believers thanks to my friend's ministry. The service was in Mandarin, so I understood nothing, but I did think the pastor, a very senior man, seemed a little boring—he was soft-spoken, a little stooped over, and preached without any expressions of excitement or emotion.

At lunch after the service, I asked the four young Christians, "Is your pastor a good preacher?" They exclaimed, "Oh yes! He is a great preacher. He spent many years in prison for Jesus Christ." Their measurement of the sermon had nothing to do with oratory ability and everything to do with a life faithfully lived in the face of suffering.

At a conference of African leaders, I listened to a testimony by a woman from Senegal. This dear sister left the faith of her village and decided to follow Jesus after he visited her in a dream. She lost her marriage, children, home, and front teeth after her family beat her. But she decided that following Jesus was worth it all, and now, over a decade later, her son is a fellow Jesus follower and together they are explaining the grace and power of Jesus Christ to their ethnic group—the very people that had persecuted her.

One of the most significant personal lessons that I have learned from our global family over these years is this: the spread of the gospel and the work of God in the world will be accomplished by people with a rugged, sacrificial faith. We need to be courageous—not fearless but rather confessing, like the psalmist who said, "*When* I am afraid, I put my trust in you" (Psalm 56:3, emphasis added). We should acknowledge our fears but not be ruled by them.

BUT I'M NOT READY

These extreme stories might motivate some of us, but others of us want to run and hide. We're not ready to follow the sacrificial life of Jesus to the point of being faithful unto death or even faithful unto prison. Where do we start?

I don't have an absolute answer; I can only encourage you to take the next step. Small sacrifices can condition us spiritually for greater sacrifices. Take the next step. Move ahead. Take a risk. Pursue someone in Jesus' name. Invite your Hindu coworker to a meal. Go on a service project to demonstrate love in an economically poorer community.

Sacrifice for some will be financial, for others it might be the use of time, for others still it might be opening our homes and giving up "private family time" over the holidays in order to welcome international students. For others it could mean serving in the legal system pro bono to defend the rights of or advocate for immigrants. For others it might mean a lifetime of service in the toughest places on earth. And most severely for some, it could mean laying down their lives.

GET OUT OF YOUR BUBBLE

When I taught at Gordon College, the students would complain at times about "the Gordon bubble."[6] When I first heard the term, I asked what they meant. They explained that living thirty miles north of Boston in a beautiful but sometimes isolated setting with people who were all supposedly Christian left them feeling like they were living an existence that was too insulated from "the real world." One student who had been raised in a rougher neighborhood of Boston told me that the campus scared him—there were no sirens, few night noises, no people yelling at each other, and a minimal number of cars on the one road that runs through the campus.

I've thought a lot about the "living in a bubble" issue, and I've come to realize that we all in effect live in some type of bubble—either by choice (as in the insulated-from-the-world tidy suburb that I live in) or by life circumstance (as in the bubble of poverty that locks people into a lifestyle that they'd never choose for themselves). Many of us find ourselves in the former type of bubbles, the ones that our wealth allows us to create for ourselves.

We have choices, but what will we choose? We can stay in the comfort zone or we can leave our bubbles and go serve and learn elsewhere (as many Gordon students do) to offset the bubble effect. We have the freedom to travel, volunteer, and reach out to internationals in our midst. The bubbles we live in are often the self-created oases of wealth and isolation with remote-controlled garage doors leading us into our air-conditioned homes. Will we choose to stay there?

Sometimes, for those of us who live middle-class American lives, the problem is that we like our bubbles. They're safe and cozy. They're predictable, manageable, and comfortable. A woman at my church once told me that she refuses to go anywhere where she might hear Jesus' name taken in vain; her insulated bubble will probably even keep her away from young Christians who bring their habits with them as they start the faith journey.

The issue for any Christ-following person is that the life of discipleship is not about safety and predictability. It's not about protecting ourselves in our bubbles. It's about risk, faith, and crossing boundaries into the unknown. As John Ortberg writes, the life of following Jesus is about getting out of the boat and trusting Jesus to take care of us on the open sea.[7]

Here's a simple example: in the bubble where my wife, Christie, and I live, nobody smokes. But several of our friends do, and when we meet with them or drive them in our cars, the smell lingers. On one occasion, I came into the house after some meetings and Christie immediately asked, "*Who* have you been with today? You smell like you've smoked two packs of cigarettes!"

When we exit our bubbles and spend time confronting the challenging needs in our world, the world inevitably gets on us—like the lingering smell of cigarette smoke. If I'm in the world (as I'm supposed to be as Jesus' disciple),

I get the world "on me." That's why I need to go regularly to a gathering of fellow Christians. Christian fellowship is where I'm supposed to come, confess my sins, and re-align my purposes with the purposes of God. I come into the corporate worship of the people of God to get "scrubbed up" spiritually, *so that* I can return the next week as a redeemed, forgiven witness for Jesus Christ.

Let's be ready and willing to leave our bubbles to do the work of being salt and light in our messy world. The words of John Henry Jowett have challenged me again and again to get out of my bubble and serve:

> It is possible to evade a multitude of sorrows through the cultivation of an insignificant life. Indeed, if a person's ambition is to avoid the troubles of life, the recipe is simple: shed your ambitions in every direction, cut the wings of every soaring purpose, and seek a life with the fewest contacts and relations. If you want to get through life with the smallest trouble, you must reduce yourself to the smallest compass. Tiny souls can dodge through life; bigger souls are blocked on every side. As soon as a person begins to enlarge his or her life, resis-tances are multiplied. Let a person remove petty selfish purposes and enthrone Christ, and sufferings will be increased on every side.[8]

The choices that we make as we seek to integrate the message of John 3:16 into our lives will grow as we im-itate the sacrificial lifestyle of Jesus.

NEXT STEPS

What is one practical way that you can imitate Jesus and do something sacrificial this week to demonstrate Jesus' love to your family and in your neighborhood, community, school, or work place? Think of sacrifice in different areas:

- A sacrifice of *time*: invest the hours needed to befriend a person, advocate for the economically poor, join a group to battle various forms of injustice, learn about other religions, give up two weeks of vacation to serve crossculturally.

- A sacrifice of *money*: give to ministries and people serving the world in ways or in places that you cannot.

- A sacrifice of *dreams*: lay aside the so-called American dream of "more" or "security" in favor of service to and love for others.

- A sacrifice of *relationships*: befriend those outside of the Christian faith who might ask awkward questions you don't know the answer to.

"HIS ONE AND ONLY SON"

JESUS: THE CENTER POINT OF SALVATION

Salvation is found in no one else, for there is no other name under heaven given to mankind by which we must be saved.

ACTS 4:12

For there is one God and one mediator between God and mankind, the man Christ Jesus, who gave himself as a ransom for all people.

1 TIMOTHY 2:5-6

E. Stanley Jones served much of his life as a missionary to India. Given that India is the birthplace of many of the other world religions (Hinduism, Buddhism, Jainism,

Sikhism), Jones fostered interfaith dialogue through what he called "Round Table Conferences." At these roundtable dialogues, religious leaders from the many faiths of India would discuss how their respective faiths responded to various issues such as sin, the problem of pain, and life after death. In one of these dialogues, Jones was asked by other religious leaders, "What does Christianity have that other religions don't have?" Jones responded succinctly, "Jesus Christ."[1]

Contrast Jones's focus on the absolute uniqueness of Jesus—the "one and only-ness" if you will—with another dialogue I participated in while registering for a conference in Delhi, India. The conference was at a secular university, so I expected little in terms of Christian presence. As I approached the person handling registrations, I noticed that she had multiple pictures of Jesus on her desk. I asked, "Are you a follower of Jesus?"

"Oh yes," she exclaimed. "He is one of my favorites."

In Hindu homes, you often find some variation of a "god shelf" that includes statues or pictures of the Hindu deities to whom the family is devoted. Ganesha (the elephant-headed deity) could be there to remove obstacles; Lakshmi is often there in hopes of bringing wealth and prosperity; Krishna often dominates as the god of compassion. The woman had added pictures of Jesus because she had read that Jesus was the god who could heal diseases.

A multi-deity "god shelf" might sound strange to those of us from Western culture, but don't we do the same thing—only perhaps without actual pictures or statues of deities? We call on Jesus when we have a great need, but we rely on our credit cards to make us comfortable and prosperous. We look to human leaders or social programs or political systems to remove obstacles. Our "God shelf" wants Jesus to share the space with other things we worship such as the priorities of comfort, convenience, and consumerism.

That dialogue in Delhi and my connecting it back to our "God shelves" point to one basic question: Can Jesus be simply *one* of our favorites, as if there is an acceptable menu of deities for us to call on depending on their special gifts or functions? When John 3:16 refers to Jesus as God's only begotten or one and only son, does that mean that Jesus wants a monopoly over our lives? And is Christian faith a Jesus-only belief system?

WHAT DOES "ONE AND ONLY SON" MEAN?

The phrase "only begotten" in the older translations of the Bible or "one and only" in the newer ones often goes without explanation as we quote John 3:16, but the words demand our attention—especially if we wrestle with the question of whether all people should be invited to salvation through Jesus Christ.

Is Jesus the only way of salvation? Are other religions incomplete, at best, and invalid, at worst? If we say yes to these questions, aren't we being presumptuous or belligerent, especially in this age of pluralism (the belief that all religions and philosophies are fundamentally okay, and none is better than another)?

Our starting point in answering these tough questions must be with the wider scriptural teachings about God and not just focus on John 3:16. The Bible affirms:

- That God alone is God and does not tolerate the worship of any other (Exodus 20:3).

- That God will not share his glory or our worship with any other—not because God is an egomaniac but because God wants us to live in the truth (Isaiah 42:8; 48:11).

- That apart from God "there is no savior" (Isaiah 43:11).

- That at the name of God, all of humanity will bow (Isaiah 45:23; Philippians 2:5-11).

Following on these biblical teachings about God as the one and only Savior/Lord/God, we can then look to the New Testament references to Jesus as the only name that saves (Acts 4:12), the only mediator between us and God (1 Timothy 2:5-6), and "the way and the truth and the life" (John 14:6). When Jesus completes that final verse, he affirms absolutely that "No one comes to the Father except through me" (John 14:6).

The reference to Jesus as God's "one and only" son uses the Greek word *monogenēs*; it is stating that Jesus literally has the "same genes" or the identical genetic makeup of God. Max Lucado elaborates, "Jesus isn't begotten in the sense that he began but in the sense that he and God have the same essence, eternal life span, unending wisdom, and tireless energy. Every quality we attribute to God, we can attribute to Jesus."[2]

Lucado and other writers point to Jesus' words that "anyone who has seen me has seen the Father" (John 14:9) and that "I and the Father are one" (John 10:30). John introduces Jesus in his Gospel as the "one and only Son" who came from God to demonstrate God's glory, grace, and truth (John 1:14). In Colossians 1:15, Paul refers to Jesus' uniqueness by referring to him as "the image of the invisible God," the creator of all things in heaven and on earth, the head of the church, the supreme Lord. The author of Hebrews writes that Jesus is "the radiance of God's glory and the exact representation" of God's nature who holds everything together by his power (Hebrews 1:3).

In short, the Bible does not leave any room for us to make Jesus "one of our favorites." He is God in human form, and everything in our gospel message revolves around him. Jesus is the only door for salvation, the only Savior, the only source for forgiveness. Jesus gives us direct access to God (Ephesians 2:18), which is why we close our prayers, "In Jesus' name, we pray."

It's no wonder that Jesus becomes the great dividing line, the stumbling block in presenting Christianity in a pluralistic world. Yet this is the message of the gospel—an invitation to a living relationship with God through Jesus Christ.

IF JESUS IS THE ONE AND ONLY . . .

If Jesus is the one and only son of God, the one and only source of salvation, the one and only Lord of creation, what does it mean for us?

If Jesus is the one and only, it provokes the personal question, is he *my* one and only? Am I listening for his voice, obeying his teaching, and living with the values and attitudes he would want? Is he the focal point of my life, finances, and future?

Think through these questions. They are not easy because many things around us want to be at the center of our lives. It's an active choice to bring all of our other options and concerns to Jesus.

One little booklet years ago shaped my answers to the question of Jesus' supremacy or lordship in my life. Robert Boyd Munger's booklet *My Heart—Christ's Home* details a parable of Jesus' visit into all the "rooms" of our lives.[3] We want to keep him in our neat and tidy living rooms where we can, in effect, put our best foot forward and give Jesus the impression of our "together" lives. But in the story, Jesus keeps wandering—into the dining room to address our appetites and desires, into the workroom to speak to our priorities, into the library and the recreation room to speak into the things that we input through reading or media, and into our closets to deal with the things we desperately want to hide. The parable concludes with the narrator transferring over the title of the house so that Jesus can become the one and only Master of the whole home.

If Jesus is the one and only, it compels us to share his life with others. As we'll discuss in the next chapter, our mission is to invite people to consider this "one and only" Savior. But since he is the only savior, our sense of urgency in our broken world intensifies. When we comprehend our unique Lord and Savior, we find ourselves in good company with Paul the apostle, compelled to share this great news (see 1 Corinthians 9:16).

If Jesus is the one and only, it takes us to a renewed commitment to making Jesus known in the world—sharing the love of God with the people across street, across cultures, or across the world. Our next chapter dives into our call to an invitational lifestyle, but it bears stating briefly here: the Bible says that we are Christ's ambassadors (2 Corinthians 5:20), and what do ambassadors do? They deliver messages from the king or president who sends the ambassadors to other nations. We are ambassadors of the kingdom of Jesus Christ, and we have a message to people across the world—that the one and only Jesus, the one and only source of salvation, is inviting every person into a unique relationship of love, forgiveness, and joy.

If Jesus is the one and only, it provokes us to wrestle with the realities of people who have never heard about Jesus Christ. We will approach this tough question in chapter eight. But we need to ask, what is the spiritual destiny of people who know nothing of God's invitation through Jesus? What will their lives look like both in this life and into eternity if no one goes to deliver this invitation?

We will explore this further in the next chapters, but I close this chapter with a quotation from Robertson McQuilkin. I consider this to be the best biblical response to the question of "people who have never heard" about this unique, one-and-only Jesus:

> We may not be able to prove from Scripture with absolute certainty that no soul since Pentecost has ever been saved by extraordinary means without the knowledge of Christ. But neither can we prove from Scripture that a single soul has been so saved. If there is an alternative [to Jesus as Savior], God has not told us of it. If God in His revelation felt it mandatory not to proffer such a hope, how much more should we refrain from theorizing. . . . So long as the truth revealed to us identifies only one way of escape, this is what we must live by and proclaim.[4]

NEXT STEPS

Challenge yourself with these questions:

- What might be occupying the place of honor in your life so that Jesus gets relegated to being "one of your favorites"?

- What attitudes in you or actions toward others might change this week if you lived out your convictions that Jesus is the one and only savior?

"THAT WHOEVER BELIEVES IN HIM"

THE INVITATION:
A RELATIONSHIP WITH GOD
THROUGH JESUS

> Whoever *unfurls 3:16 as a banner for the ages.*
> Whoever *rolls out the welcome mat of heaven to*
> *humanity.* Whoever *invites the world to God.*
>
> **MAX LUCADO**

I magine that you are part of the followers of Christ in the first century, shortly after Jesus' resurrection and ascension into heaven. You live in Damascus and worship with a small band of disciples there. And imagine that you became a follower of Jesus because you had heard John or Peter preaching an invitation to faith based on the message of what we now call John 3:16 (by the mid-first century, the truth of John 3:16 would have easily circulated through the church, but it most likely did not exist in the form we have now). When you heard the "whoever" in this invitation—the idea that every person was invited—you believed.

Now go further: imagine that information has spread in Damascus that Saul of Tarsus, the man who supervised the stoning death of Stephen, was on his way to your city with authorization from the religious leaders to find and persecute the followers of this Jesus, the one who claimed to be the Messiah. While you are praying and bringing your fears to God, the Lord speaks.

As you listen, the Lord gives you the instructions to go to a certain house to look for Saul, who, according to the Lord, is praying. You remind the Lord that Saul is a very bad man sent to arrest and imprison Christians. But the Lord responds and tells you that this persecutor is now the Lord's choice instrument to preach the gospel to the Gentile world, kings, and the children of Israel.

Now you hear the word "whoever" in John 3:16 from an entirely new angle. "Whoever" includes you, and now "whoever" includes Saul of Tarsus, a first century religious extremist dedicated to creating terror in the church. God so loved Saul that "whoever"—including him—believes can come into a relationship with Jesus.

In this imaginary journey, you have been living in something of the tensions Ananias must have experienced as God called him to go, find, and pray for Saul of Tarsus, the persecutor turned evangelist who we know today as Paul the apostle (see Acts 9). We can assume that Ananias, empowered by the Holy Spirit, grasped the "whoever" open door of God's invitation because he obeys God and goes to the place where Saul is staying, lays his hands on him, and calls him "Brother Saul" (Acts 9:17).

The "whoever" open heart of God was now Ananias's open heart. After Saul supervises the stoning death of Stephen (Acts 7:54-60), he encounters Jesus in a vision and then Ananias visits him (Acts 9:1-19). By Acts 9:20 he is in the synagogue preaching that Jesus is indeed the Son of God.

Whoever—no matter age, gender, ethnicity, socio-economic status, nationality, sinful past, or broken life—is invited to a living and dynamic relationship with God through Jesus. And Saul/later Paul would become the primary messenger of this invitation in the first century, traveling widely as he is motivated by the zealous desire that every person, every "whoever" receives an invitation to this relationship (see Romans 15:20).

Max Lucado summarizes it beautifully: "The word [whoever] sledgehammers racial fences and dynamites social classes. It bypasses gender borders and surpasses ancient traditions. *Whoever* makes it clear: God exports his grace worldwide. For those who attempt to restrict it, Jesus has a word: *Whoever*."[1]

INVITING ALL THE "WHOEVERS" TO JESUS

When my friend Jack defined *evangelicals* as "the people that are always pointing their fingers at everyone else telling us all the things that are wrong with us," I was mortified. I wondered, *Is that really the way we are seen?*

Maybe the issue relates to the way that many of us see the task of evangelism or sharing the good news about Jesus. Is evangelism something we do *at* people, or is evangelism a lifestyle of friendship, engagement, and life-sharing with others? Is it proclaiming answers, or is it provoking questions that invite people to contemplate what it's like to have a living and real relationship with God? Is it first and foremost denouncing sin, or is it first inviting people to the mercy of God and the forgiveness found in Jesus? Is it condemning people to hell or inviting people to eternal life?

Perhaps my questions are too polarizing, because sharing the gospel does at times involve preaching, proc-lamation, calling out sin, and warning of judgment (see chapter 8), but our first mission is to be inviters by wel-coming people to know the Jesus that we know.

LIVING OUT THE INVITATION OF JOHN 3:16

How can we live as invitational people? Here are ten sug-gestions, most of which are practical and common sense, but bear repeating because they present a real way to live the gospel message through our lifestyles.

Learn to ask good questions. When we look at the Gospels and the ministry of Jesus, it's amazing how often

Jesus asked questions or even answered questions with questions. In discussion with people who are outside of the Christian family of faith, I often ask, "Is there any faith component in your life?" or "What do you do in the face of crises or in a circumstance you cannot control?" Asked graciously and nonjudgmentally, the answers to these questions can give us insight into the friendships we are building. The answers might reveal the areas of their lives to which Jesus' invitation might mean the most.

Practice hospitality. Much of Jesus' teaching in the New Testament happened around the table, perhaps because hospitality can help lower people's defenses. In addition—at least in my area of the world (Boston) where the people I meet are secularized and often suspicious of so-called evangelicals—a meal together can help people see that we Christians are quite normal, eat normal food, and even have interests beyond church life.

Demonstrate love. In many places where the gospel message has been heard, people need to see the gospel in action. My colleague Jack told me he'd never come to church, but if we were building housing in a slum, he'd be delighted to join me. Demonstrated love toward the economically needy, to the refugee, or social outcast (and to all the categories of people Jesus mentions in Matthew 25:31-46), advertises the fact that our faith demonstrates itself in active love and compassion.

Understand in order to be understood. Too often we offer the biblical answers before we know what the questions are. Asking good questions (see my first point) and listening can instruct us on how to express God's invitation. In a world where almost all of us have exposure to people whose worldviews are shaped by Islam, Hinduism, Buddhism, or some other belief system, we need to understand what people believe so that we can understand points about Christianity that might be confusing. Did you know that many Muslims believe that Christians think that the Trinity is God the father, Mary the mother, and Jesus the son? Or did you know that the Buddhist "First Noble Truth" is that "all of life contains suffering"? How do we explain abundant life (John 10:10) to that person?[2] It's better to explain your beliefs *after* you understand theirs.

Invite people into your pain. In our book *Fellowship of the Suffering*, Dave Ripper and I refer to "evangelistic suffering" because the Christian response to pain, cancer, death, and loss often demonstrates a supernatural peace and hope.

Join people in their pain. At the hospital laboratory where my wife, Christie, worked for forty years, every coworker knew about her Christian faith, but seldom asked—until they were facing a crisis themselves. They would come to her (I referred to her as the "pastor of the lab") for counsel, comfort, and even prayer—after a college-aged son died, after a partner was diagnosed with cancer, after a myriad of marriage and family conflicts. Their pain became a bridge for Christie's compassion and perspective of hope.

Listen to their critiques of the Christian community. Maybe this is just my perspective from living in Boston, but it seems that some of the most "publicly Christian" people in the news can be distractions that complicate our efforts to share our faith. My instinctive response is to get defensive when people ask questions about the moral failures of a Christian TV personality, or the far right or left political views of people who profess Christ, or the controversial comments by Christians in the media about immigrants, creation, or the environment. But I need to listen to these critiques, and I often end up openly admitting to others that the Christian team is far from perfect and far from unified. People need to know that we don't see every issue in the same way, and I have found that it adds credibility to our Christian thoughtfulness.

Be a friend, not a salesperson. Many books and seminars advocate "friendship evangelism," but the friendship is often portrayed as a means-to-an-end friendship that may or may not survive if the person does not respond affirmatively to the gospel. Faithful friendships might not get the fastest results—indeed, they may not get any results—but our faithfulness can demonstrate to others the ongoing pursuit of God for these friends.

Go into their world. Too often, we want to invite people into our world: our Christmas or Easter church services, our investigative Bible study, or our Alpha classes. These might be wonderful avenues for inviting people to faith, but what about all the people who aren't inclined to come into our worlds? We need to find ways to integrate our faith into our time at work, our hobbies, or our love of sports. We need to go back to chapter two, "'For God': God, the Great Pursuer," to look for ways to bring our Christian lives to the places where the "whoevers" live.

Be gracious in disagreement. In addition to learning to disagree more civilly with each other, we need to learn an even greater civility in our discussions with people outside of our family of faith. Good dialogue and good friendships will inevitably lead to the expression of opposing views and ideas contrary to Christian faith. In this regard, consider Paul when he was in Athens (Acts 17:16-34). The Bible states that the presence of the multiple statues and altars of false gods deeply troubled or provoked Paul's spirit (Acts 17:16). He probably wanted to call out their idolatry, but instead, he spoke graciously, affirmed the deep spirituality he observed as he walked around (Acts 17:23), referred to their statues, and even quoted from their writings (Acts 17:28). His first goal was to engage them, understand their context, and even use one of their statues to invite them to Jesus Christ.

THE BOTTOM LINE

God has made us inviters to the global "whoevers" who don't yet know about Jesus. We are inviting them to believe in a person, Jesus. John's use of the phrase "believe" is almost always "believe in" or "believe into" because he's not referring to doctrine or a belief system. He is referring to a living relationship with the one we believe in—Jesus Christ!

84

We have no need to coerce or manipulate; we simply can invite people to believe in the love of God as expressed through the life-giving sacrifice of Jesus Christ. The fact that our mission is invitation takes the pressure off us—*we* don't save people. We present them with Jesus Christ and then let them decide for themselves.

NEXT STEPS

- Go back to chapter four ("'The World': The Target of God's Love") and stop and pray for an unreached people group that has not yet been invited to understand the love of God through Jesus Christ.

- Review the ten lifestyle ideas in this chapter that relate to ways to invite all the "whoevers" to Jesus. Choose to act on one or two of them in the next week.

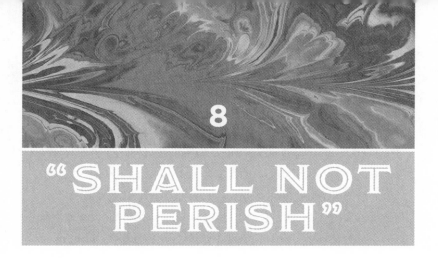

8

"SHALL NOT PERISH"

THE WARNING:
TO ESCAPE CONDEMNATION

*The vague and tenuous hope that God is too kind
to punish the ungodly has become a deadly
opiate for the consciences of millions.*

A. W. TOZER

I first met Rocco Collazzo in 1977 when I arrived at his home in Cambridge, Massachusetts, to pick up my date, Christie, Rocco's daughter. When I saw the name plate above the doorbell, I cowered a little. I confess that I, coming from my Scottish-English-Irish heritage, did some name-related stereotyping. I envisioned that some large, muscular, tough-looking fellow would meet me at the door with a scowl and the question, "Whaadya want with my dawter?"

I pressed the doorbell and Rocco answered. He was at least six inches shorter than me, and he was a long way from muscular and tough-looking. If you met him, saw his smile, or heard him laugh, you'd be more likely to give him a hug than run in fear. I grew to love Rocco over the next twenty-three years, and he loved me, because not only did he become a father-figure to me but also became my father-in-law.

Rocco had abandoned any evidence of Christian faith years before. Another daughter was born severely handicapped, and his pastor told him that it was "because of his sins." If God was that cruel, Rocco reasoned he wanted no part of him.

Christie and I loved Rocco, looked for ways to serve, and talked openly about our faith. We hoped he could see the love of Jesus through us. Rocco often supported our international ministry because he respected our service to the poor, but he resisted any move toward personal faith.

As he aged, our concern for his relationship with God intensified. We wanted Rocco to know God's love, experience a vital relationship with Jesus, and anticipate eternal life even after death. We repeatedly offered him the invitation to believe, but he repeatedly resisted.

One evening, the phrase "shall not perish" echoed in our minds as we prepared to have dinner with Rocco.[1] We always wanted to talk about God's love, forgiveness, and offer of eternal life, but this night we remembered that John 3:16 (and elsewhere in John 3) carried in it the reality of "perishing" or what the Bible calls "judgment" (Hebrews 9:27).

We all hope that everyone will receive the eternal life mentioned in John 3:16, but somehow we manage to overlook John 3:18: "Whoever believes in him is not condemned, but whoever does not believe stands condemned already because they have not believed in the name of God's one and only Son." Or move down to John 3:36: "Whoever believes in the Son has eternal life, but whoever rejects the Son will not see life, for God's wrath remains on them." A negative response to the invitation to believe in Jesus has an eternal consequence: judgment.

So on this night, Christie and I decided to try to take the conversation with Rocco in a different direction. We reiterated the good news of God's love through Jesus Christ, but we introduced the idea of the judgment of sins, the justice and holiness of God, and the biblical teaching on the realities of eternal separation from God: hell.

The conversation escalated at times, and Rocco offered the typical pushback: "What about evil in the world? I've lived a better life than most, so I'm okay. What about people who have never heard about Jesus? And what happens to people from other religions?"

We tried to steer the conversation back to Rocco's own response to the invitation of God, but he shut the conversation down with this statement: "If there is a God who allows people to go to hell, I would never want to spend eternity with him. *I choose hell*."

We were stunned. Saddened. Confused as to what to say next. I wanted to second-guess the biblical teaching concerning the eternal impact of our earthly choices about Jesus. Even the greatest optimist struggles to know how to respond when a person states clearly, "I choose hell." The personal realization of a loved one's choice of hell can wreak havoc on one's theological system and worldview.

Our invitation to Rocco to understand the love of Jesus and eternal life continued, but the conversation that night with Rocco combined with the "shall not perish" of John 3:16 provoked questions in us:

- What does the Bible *actually* teach about hell and judgment? (I'm convinced that instead of examining the biblical teaching, many get their "theology" of hell and judgment from a combination of horror movies, Halloween stories, and Dante Alighieri's *The Divine Comedy* or John Milton's *Paradise Lost*.)

- Can people be saved outside of a relationship with Jesus?

- Does God's love overrule his judgment so that people get forgiven even when they resist him?

- Are there any chances of salvation after death?

- Doesn't this idea of Jesus as the "only way to God" seem too exclusive?[2]

ENGAGED EXCLUSIVISTS

Is Jesus the only way, so that those who never know or never respond affirmatively to his invitation get condemned to hell? Is Robertson McQuilkin correct—that the Bible offers us no alternative to Jesus as the "one and only" Savior?

Timothy Tennent, a missiologist, theologian, and expert on world religions, identifies the Christian position of Jesus' unique capacity to save as *exclusivism*. He writes that the Bible affirms three non-negotiables built around the unique person and life of Jesus Christ:

- Exclusivists affirm the unique authority of Jesus Christ as the apex of revelation and the norm by which all other beliefs must be critiqued.

- Exclusivists affirm that the Christian faith centers around the proclamation of the historical death and resurrection of Jesus Christ as the decisive event in human history.

- Exclusivists believe that salvation comes through repentance and faith in Christ's work on the cross and that no one can be saved without an explicit act of repentance and faith based on the knowledge of Christ.[3]

The exclusivism of Christian faith and the belief that Jesus is the only way of salvation does not place us in a superior posture where we celebrate our salvation and ignore those who have not responded. In John 3:16, "God so loved the world" and "whoever believes" comes in combination together with "shall not perish" as our calling to be engaged in our world through friendships, service, sacrifice, and dialogue. Tennent refers to this as being "engaged exclusivists." [4] Engaged exclusivists live with two distinctives in our approach to people from other religions or worldviews.

First, we go looking for "the fingerprint of God" in these religious beliefs, worldviews, or philosophies. God's common grace is evident in both the cultures of the world and in other worldviews as preparation for the gospel. The sense of God's "divine nature" Paul refers to in Romans 1:20 or the "loving memory" of God even in unbelievers as described by St. Augustine in *Confessions*, points to the pursuing God revealing himself to draw people toward a relationship through Jesus Christ.[5]

Second, our biblical understanding of judgment, hell, or perishing should compel us to greater outreach, engagement, and involvement with our world. The reality of judgment is not an invitation for Christ-followers to become judgmental. Instead, it's a call to greater urgency to share Jesus' love, greater compassion, and greater sacrifice so that everyone has a chance to respond to God's invitation.

Al Tizon warns us "that any notion of the gospel that is primarily motivated by fear, pharisaical legalism, and/or hellfire-and-brimstone preaching dangerously flirts with the gospel of hate."[6] In other words, if we turn the balance of God's love and justice into a focus on judgment and condemnation, our message can degenerate into self-righteousness and a message that communicates "God wants to damn you to hell" rather than "God loves you."

Tizon strikes a biblically balanced summary when he writes:

> The church should not avoid declaring God's judgment on sin—because, again, at the base of this gospel lies the holiness of God and the call to repentance—but listeners need to hear it in the larger context of the truly good news that God so loved that God decided to dwell among us in Jesus Christ for our salvation (John 1:1-3, 14; 3:16). It is this gospel, and not the gospel of hate, that God in Christ has called us to embody and proclaim for the sake of the world.[7]

"SHALL NOT PERISH"

John 3:17 reminds us that God sent Jesus into the world not to condemn the world but to save the world through him. John 3:16-17 is what we'd all prefer to believe: that Jesus' love conquers everything and that everyone will live eternally with God in heaven.

But the phrase "shall not perish" in John 3:16 calls that conclusion into question because even the great invitation of God in this verse calls for a response: "whoever believes in him." And if we still have our hopes up, John's summary at the end of chapter three closes that door: "Whoever believes in the Son has eternal life, but whoever rejects the Son will not see life, for God's wrath remains on them" (John 3:36).

Why do we prefer not to discuss the realities of judgment or hell? After all, the Bible teaches the reality of hell just as it does the reality of heavenly eternal life. Without Jesus' sacrificial life paying the penalty for our sins and absorbing the judgment of our righteous God for sin and rebellion, we face judgment on our own. We need to remember that the love and sacrifice of Jesus is offered in juxtaposition to the realities of our being lost in our trespasses and sins: "All have sinned and fall short of the glory of God" (Romans 3:23) and "The wages of sin is death" (Romans 6:23).

Jesus did not come to condemn us—we were *already* condemned! God is righteous; sin will be judged; and without a substitute to take our place, we find ourselves under God's wrath. God gives us one life to live and after this comes judgment, according to Hebrews 9:27. This summary sounds more like bad news, right? In contrast, the message of John 3:16 is why the gospel is called good news! Jesus has taken our place. Sin has been judged on the cross. When Jesus said, "It is finished" (John 19:30) he used a term that we use in the business world—the debt has been paid in full. The good news is that in Christ, we don't need to suffer the judgment for our sins. The words of an old hymn describe the saving work of the pursuing God this way:

Jesus sought me when a stranger,
 wandering from the fold of God;

he, to rescue me from danger,
bought me with his precious blood.
Oh, to grace how great a debtor
daily I'm constrained to be![8]

SHALL NOT PERISH—IMPLICATIONS

I met over breakfast with an older Christian brother who has served as a mentor in my life for more than forty years. He—always the gracious, non-condemning pastor—looked concerned when I referred to my burden for the lostness of people without Jesus Christ. I think he was concerned that my burden could drift into self-righteous judgmentalism or the harsh theology of someone who almost seems to revel at the idea of condemnation of people from lifestyles, religions, or worldviews different than my own.

He asked, "Don't you think God's love will triumph in the end, and he'll save people in ways we don't understand on this side of eternity?"

I responded, "Wow, that's what I really want to believe, Pastor, but unfortunately, I don't find anything in the Bible that supports that optimistic notion." I added (perhaps because I serve with many others who choose hardships by taking the invitation of God to others in difficult, often poor, and sometimes violent locations across the world), "In addition, if all of these folks are going to be 'saved in ways we don't understand this side of eternity,' why would people want to make these types of sacrifices?"

We parted ways probably disagreeing on this point, but I am convinced: first, if the love of God is not enough to provoke us to share the good news of Jesus' love and life given for us, then perhaps we need to consider also the reality of eternal condemnation that people face without him. Second, the thought that "there is some other way" that people without Jesus will enter eternal life needs to be seriously tested by careful Bible study. And third, as gospel proclaimers, we need a good news message that is not afraid of warning.

KEEP LOVING ROCCO

Our warning conversation with my father-in-law took place in 1993. He seemed to have made a final, painful decision ("I choose hell")—but we, especially my wife, persevered in prayer and kept inviting him to God's love as demonstrated by us. We helped him through illness, worked to maintain his home, assisted in managing his financial affairs, comforted him through the death of his son, and invited him into our lives.

In early 2000, we had another deep conversation with Rocco. His diabetes was progressing and his kidneys were failing. We knew (and we think he knew) that his time on earth was coming to an end. He had been hospi- talized and we went to see him in the intensive care unit. We had planned our visit before we went: Christie would pray and I would speak. After some hugs, kisses, and tears, I asked him:

"Rocco, do you know that you're dying?"

"Yea," he mumbled quietly.

"Would you like to go to heaven and be with Jesus?" I asked.

He shrugged his shoulders and turned away. Normally, this was my cue to give up, but I sensed the Lord telling me to ask again. I repeated:

"Rocco, do you know that you're dying?"

"Yes."

"Would you like to go to heaven and be with Jesus?"

This time he looked at me and said, "Okay."

"Then just say this simple prayer: 'Jesus, have mercy.'"

Rocco prayed! For the first time I could ever remember. He said, "Jesus, have mercy on my soul; Jesus, have mercy on my soul; Jesus, have mercy on my soul."

His countenance eased and a sense of peace flooded the room. He had expanded my suggested prayer. And he had repeated it three times. I'm convinced God directed the words of his prayer so my wife and I could be confident that this prayer was *his*. And I'm convinced that he said it three times so that we would have no doubt that he had prayed it.

Twenty-three years of love and prayers from me, a lifetime of love and prayers from Christie. God's pursuing love never gave up on Rocco. We never stopped inviting him. And finally he said yes.

NEXT STEPS

- Are you ready to devote some time to understanding what the Bible says about hell and judgment? See note two in this chapter for some suggested readings.

- Is there a Rocco in your life that needs prayer? Ask God if this is the time for a gentle warning.

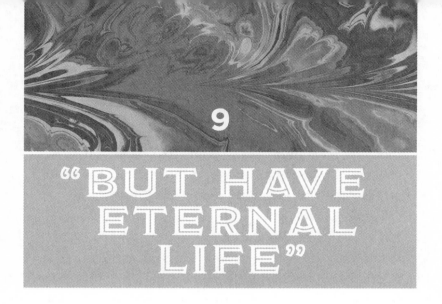

9

"BUT HAVE ETERNAL LIFE"

THE GOAL: A LIVING, VITAL, ETERNAL RELATIONSHIP WITH GOD

Now this is eternal life: that they know you, the only true God, and Jesus Christ, whom you have sent.

JOHN 17:3

In preparation for writing this chapter, I asked ten fellow Christians of various ages and church backgrounds, "When I say the words *eternal life*, what comes to mind?" Most answered "heaven" or "life with Jesus after death."

Many of us do associate eternal life with something that happens after our earthly, physical life ends. We breathe our last breath, our heart stops, and we enter eternal life. Or, if we are from the tradition of Adventist theology, we enter a state called "soul sleep" where we stay until Jesus comes for the "resurrection of the dead," and we are resurrected to eternal life. The messages at Christian funerals often state or imply that the deceased has now entered eternal life.

Life after death offers great comfort and assurance, but that's not how Jesus defined eternal life. In his prayer recorded in John 17:3, Jesus gives a very specific definition: "This is eternal life, that they know you, the only true God, and Jesus Christ, whom you sent."

In other words, eternal life commences when we enter into a personal relationship with God through Jesus Christ. Put another way and joining it with Jesus' interchange with Nicodemus in John 3, if we begin our physical lives when we are born, we launch into eternal life when we are "born again" (John 3:3).

ETERNAL LIFE BEGINS NOW

We come into relationship with God through belief in Jesus and what he has done for us, and eternal life begins. We invite others to believe and they respond—thus eternal life begins for them. The goal of living an invitational life, the goal of inviting people across cultures to believe, is that they too can enter into eternal life: a living, vital, relationship with God.

A few years ago, I had the privilege of entering into dialogue with Mustafa, a medical doctor from Libya who was interning in cardiology at a Boston hospital. I invited him to dinner and we met at a restaurant near the hospital. After we ordered our meal, I said to Mustafa, "I'm a Christian, and I pause before eating to say a prayer of thanks for the food. Do you do that too, as a devout Muslim?" (I always give friends from other religious backgrounds the benefit of the doubt that they are devout.)

"Yes, of course I do," Mustafa responded.

"Then please pray."

He lifted his hands a little and said, "Bismillah," an Islamic phrase meaning "in the name of Allah" used often by Muslims to make themselves aware of Allah's presence.

A few weeks later, Mustafa invited me to his home for a meal (in many world cultures, guests are honored by being invited into the home, which is unlike US culture where a person may be honored by taking them to a restaurant). As we sat to eat, he said, "Paul, when we met before, you asked me to say thank you to Allah for the food in a Muslim way, so tonight I want to ask you to say thank you for the food in a Christian way."

I thanked him for the privilege, but I responded, "Mustafa, when I pray, I'm going to talk with God like I know him, and my familiarity with God and the one you call the prophet Isa [Jesus' name in the Qur'an] might seem to be a blasphemy to you." I was trying to explain to him the idea of what a living relationship with God could look like.

Mustafa looked shocked at the idea of blasphemy taking place in his house, so he quickly lifted his hands, said "Bismillah," and began to eat. There was no Christian prayer, but my explanation became a great conversation starter on whether Allah could be known, whether sins could be covered by another, and who Jesus is revealed to be in the Christian Bible.

WHAT IS ETERNAL LIFE?

If the term *eternal life* describes a living, vital, now-and-forever relationship with God through Jesus Christ, we need to know how to explain it—both for our own understanding and for those we invite into a similar relationship.

In John 17:3, Jesus describes it as knowing God and Jesus Christ whom God has sent. Later in John's Gospel, he talks about "abiding" or "remaining," phrases that imply a life of 24-7 total reliance on, listening to, and obedience of Jesus (see John 15). Pastor and author Eugene Peterson describes this relationship as a "long obedience in the same direction."[1] Paul the apostle refers to it as knowing Christ—he wants "to know the power of his resurrection and participation in his sufferings" (Philippians 3:10). Many others describe this living relationship with Jesus as a journey, pilgrimage, or sojourn.

Although it is tough to nail down an exact definition, the adjectives *living*, *vital*, and *eternal* all help us explore the term further.

Living. Our relationship with Jesus is not a one-time prayer followed by silence until after death. It is daily and involves listening to the Scriptures, praying about everything, and actively cultivating our awareness that Jesus, by his Spirit, is walking with us through every challenge, hardship, and opportunity of life. The phrases "don't fear," "fear not," or "don't be afraid" appear more than any other command in the Bible, and the most dominant phrase from God that follows this imperative is the promise "for I am with you." Living in relationship with Jesus doesn't mean we will never be afraid. It simply means that we can face every fear with the knowledge that Jesus is with us: "When I am afraid, I put my trust in you" (Psalm 56:3).

Vital. Later in John's Gospel, Jesus says that he has come to give us life "to the full" (John 10:10). Jesus wants our relationship with him to be abundant, meaningful, and growing. It means allowing him to stretch us and take us through new chapters of life that we might never undertake if not for our relationship with him. Paul Tournier, a Christian Swiss psychologist, summarizes vitality when he writes, "Life is an adventure directed by God."[2]

Eternal. The adventure begins with belief and trust. We entrust ourselves to Jesus and live with the assurance that what we experience now in this life with Jesus is only a partly obscured vision of what is to come. Paul the apostle describes eternal life now as seeing things "in a mirror dimly" (1 Corinthians 13:12 ESV). In one of his letters, John the apostle writes that the day is coming when we will become like Jesus because we "shall see him as he is" (1 John 3:2). As we journey on this pilgrimage that is eternal life, the more we see Jesus accurately as we read, pray, listen, and obey, the more potential we have of becoming like him, "transformed into his image" (2 Corinthians 3:18).

LIVING ETERNAL LIFE ACCORDING TO JOHN 3:16

John 3:16 itself can demonstrate what this living relationship with God through Jesus looks like. Walking daily in that eternal-life relationship includes all of the component themes we've already examined in the verse.

We live a pursuing life. We celebrate that God pursued us, and out of the overflow of that relationship, we pursue others in Jesus' name. We start to see other people as precious human beings that Jesus wants to invite into a relationship with him—invited through us!

Think of it this way: How would our vision of the people we see every day be transformed if we first saw them as men and women created in the *imago Dei,* "the image of God"? Would we learn the name of the homeless person that we bypass on the way to work so that we could greet him every day and maybe breathe a prayer for him? Would we learn greetings in other languages so that we could be a touch of grace to that new immigrant neighbor, the refugee working at the 7-Eleven, and the person from another religion in our circle of relationships? Would we awaken to the reality that these image bearers have been brought into our path by the pursuing God?

In the humorous movie *The Best Exotic Marigold Hotel*, Maggie Smith plays Muriel Donnelly, a cranky British retiree living in a dilapidated hotel in Jaipur, India. She is wheelchair-bound so the hotel staff assigns a Dalit (out-caste) woman to care for her. The woman invites Muriel to her home so that her whole family can meet her. Muriel goes with a translator because the Dalit woman and her family don't speak English. When the Dalit woman showers Muriel with food and hospitality, Muriel asks the translator why. The translator responds, "Because you have been kind to her." Muriel shamefully responds, "But I haven't been kind." The translator responds, "You're the only one who acknowledges her."[3]

For a poor, Dalit woman, the fact that Muriel saw her and talked with her—even though it was more *at* her—was an acknowledgment of her worth and their common humanity. When we go out as pursuers in eternal relationship with Jesus, we start to see people no one else sees, like Jesus with children, the sick, the Samaritan, the Gentile, and the leper. God's heart becomes our heart.

We live a loving life. We go out every day amazed at God's unconditional love for us and looking to reflect and demonstrate that love to those we touch. Maybe it starts with an act of kindness, observing and responding to a person in need. Perhaps we enter the week with a spirit of loving forgiveness toward the coworker who, for her mistake, blamed us last week in front of the boss. Perhaps it is becoming, like Christie in her micro lab, the "pastor" to hurting people in our midst.

We live a global life. We grow daily in our understanding of God's love and heart for the whole world and then let it transform the way that we look at the world, both near and far. We develop a curiosity to learn more about the world beyond our continent, realizing that North America is only about 7 percent of the world's population, according to the United Nations. As we understand God's love for the world, we are transformed in the way we view ourselves in the world as ambassadors of Christ.

We grow deeper in our understanding of Jesus' sacrifice for us. And, as we do, we respond to his sacrifice by being willing to sacrifice for the sake of others. Our vitality with Jesus gets fueled by a spirit of generosity with time, finances, or our homes. We stop worrying about what the neighbors think and we invite Mohammed and his family to a meal at our home. We relinquish some vacation time to serve on a short-term learning and service trip with a partner ministry in Guatemala. Imitating Jesus' sacrifice reshapes our generosity of life and slowly but surely weans us of some of our selfishness (see Philippians 2:3-11). We even start walking through our hardships with Jesus as he allows tough circumstances to shape us (see Psalm 119:67, 71) and see God in a way we've never seen him before (see Job 42:5).

We turn our attention daily to Jesus as the one and only Lord of our lives. We choose every day to listen first to his voice over the myriad of other voices calling for our attention. The Holy Spirit enables us to hear God say, "Go greet her," or "Build the bridge," or "Give that homeless fellow ten dollars," or "Help that man who mows your lawn get his documents in order."

We will evaluate these ongoing actions to live out John 3:16 in the final chapter, but the bottom line comes to this: as we reflect on God's love and the gift of eternal life, we look for opportunities to invite others to this same relationship. We realize the justice and holiness of God means that sin will be punished, but because we know that Jesus absorbed that penalty on the cross, we desire daily to invite others to belief in Jesus so they too may escape condemnation. And we live in the relationship that Jesus calls "eternal life"—growing in our knowledge of God, listening to his Word, and moving in obedience in that same direction. And we live with the assurance that one day "eternal life" means moving to the heavenly, perfected realm, where we will see Jesus fully.

NEXT STEPS

Think of three opportunities in the week ahead where you can:

- Acknowledge a fellow human being, created in the image of God, who no one else seems to acknowledge, and greet them by name: a homeless person, a person from another culture who works in the service industry, a lonely coworker, or a fellow student.

■ Look for an opportunity to love "the world" by doing something simple to reach out across cultures: eat a new food, learn a greeting in another language, listen to someone's "how I came to this country" story.

■ Pray for an opportunity to explain to someone else God's invitation from John 3:16.

10

THE CHALLENGE

LIVING A JOHN 3:16 LIFESTYLE

There is a you-shaped hole in God's Kingdom. Find it and fill it.

PATRICK JOHNSTONE

Remember how we started our exploration of John 3:16? Let's go back to the beginning. *God's mission in the world includes you.* Uniquely you. Specifically you. Indeed, we have been recipients of God's love, and now we serve as ambassadors of his message to the world. The Lord of the universe has a mission that includes us!

- We pursue others because God pursued us.
- We love because he first loved us.
- We enlarge our vision because our Lord loves the world.

- We're willing to sacrifice in imitation of the sacrifices he made for us.
- Our lives and our message center on Jesus Christ as "the one and only."
- We're the couriers inviting people to believe and receive the gift of eternal life.
- We're the warning lights inviting people to escape the condemnation we all deserve as sinners.
- We live daily and forever in a living, vital, eternal relationship with God.

Even though we were familiar with John 3:16 before, we now see a depth of meaning in the words that we might have overlooked in the past. But understanding the fullness of the gospel as expressed in John 3:16 is only the starting point—now the challenge is to live it out.

Reviewing John 3:16 can go in several directions. We might go back to the days when Jesus walked the earth and use that as a historical starting point to remember not only his love and sacrifice but also the love and sacrifices of those who went before us.

Or perhaps we can look forward to the day when people from every tribe and nation and language are worshiping (see Revelation 5:9 and 7:9), and we'll be motivated to enter each new day with the realization that God is bringing his kingdom, and we get to play a part in that process.

Whether it's looking for ways to bring the sacrificial love of Jesus into our communities or reflecting each morning on the fact that all that we do is in response to God's love for us, the bottom line is that John 3:16 calls us to respond. Like the prophet Isaiah, we hear God's question, "Whom shall I send? And who will go for us?" and we respond, "Here I am. Send me!" (see Isaiah 6:1-8).

LEARNING TO SWIM

When Christie and I first started dating, I couldn't swim. I could dog paddle around a little, but lap swimming was out of the question. The thought of swimming a mile (seventy-two lengths in the local pool) overwhelmed me, and the thought of open-ocean swimming made me nauseous.

My fear of water and inability to swim caused a problem: I wanted to impress this young lady I was dating, but she worked at a pool and routinely swam forty lengths (a little over a half mile) three to five times a week. Now, she wanted me to learn to swim so that we could spend more time together.

I resisted, but she was patient. She took me to a kiddie pool to practice putting my face in the water, blowing bubbles, and turning my head to breathe. Imagine my mortification as I blew bubbles, coughed on water I had swallowed, and hesitantly put my face in the water— along with the four-year-olds in my end of the pool!

Christie persisted, and I started to learn to swim. She would swim her forty lengths in about the same time as it took me to do four. Sometimes I joked that the pool level was going down based on the amount of water I swallowed! But we continued. She moved to fifty-four lengths (three-fourths of a mile); I moved to eighteen lengths (one-fourth of a mile). The goal was to swim a mile. She achieved that goal about four months after we started; I reached the goal about a year after blowing bubbles. Now, forty years married and counting, our goal together is to swim three times a week, one mile each time. And on top of this, we choose open-ocean swimming whenever possible.

So why am I telling you a nice learning-to-swim story? Because we need to start where we are and build from there.

Putting John 3:16 into action by taking the radical risk of moving to some dangerous place to share about Jesus might sound like asking us to start swimming by competing in the 2.4-mile, rough open-ocean swim of Hawaii's Ironman triathlon—after biking 112 miles and running a marathon. And giving away 50 percent of our resources to live out John 3:16 sounds like being asked to swim in the Olympics. Volunteering in our company to take the job assignment in Azerbaijan (which is 96.9 percent Muslim, according to *The World Factbook 2019*) conjures up images of swimming the English Channel (59°F/15°C or less and twenty-one miles across).

Christie didn't teach me to swim by pushing me into the deep end to see how I'd do. She didn't compare my miserable thrashing to the power strokes of the college swim team that shared the pool. And she encouraged me along the way.

So let's think of ways to get started. Here is a range of exercises that we can take in imitation of the John 3:16 life of Jesus.

GET STARTED IN THE SHALLOW END

As God calls us to join him in his global mission, his grace meets us where we are. We can make steps along the way, building our capacities as we go. To change analogies, paratroopers do not start building their skills by jumping out of a plane. They start by jumping off platforms, getting used to the parachutes, and addressing their fears of height from the ground.[1]

Being a John 3:16 person does not start with us "loving the world" by getting on a jet and leaving for the remotest jungles of Papua New Guinea or the Amazon rainforest to do Bible translation. Instead, it might start with learning about nations such as Papua New Guinea or Brazil, or learning about the work of groups that serve in linguistics or language learning in those countries.

Grab a meal, start a conversation. Pursuing others, loving the world, and sacrificing for the sake of others can start with going out to eat food from other cultures. Within ten miles of our home, Christie and I have met Buddhists at the Thai restaurant, Muslims at the Lebanese restaurant, Hindus at the Indian restaurant, and Shinto adherents at the Japanese restaurant. And when we go out, we have a few questions in mind so that we can express interest in the persons serving us and in the religious culture that has shaped their lives.

Go to a citizenship ceremony. Watching people from other lands come into our countries can be an amazing learning experience. Rationalizing that "Since I am not headed overseas, I need not have an interest in anyplace other than my home culture" misses the opportunity to learn in our ever-shrinking global village, especially if we live close to any urban center.

Survey the neighborhood. Get your town census and see if it lists things such as languages spoken. Maybe the local high school can help. Large universities often have large numbers of international students. And as these data points become known, they can fuel prayer and an openness to God that says, "Seeking Lord, what should I do with this information?" Prayer might be the first step, but there might be more.

Go together. One of the things that helped me learn to swim was that Christie took me with her. Go with someone else, maybe someone more experienced, to the restaurant, university, or English as a Second Language (ESL) class. I met Bobby for coffee at a local restaurant. Moussa, the Muslim owner and a new citizen from Egypt, came to say hello because we had talked before. I introduced him to Bobby and shared that we were both Jesus followers (Moussa already knew I was).

Generally speaking, I have found that many people from religious backgrounds such as Buddhism, Islam, or Hinduism are delighted to talk about their faith because they come from religious contexts where personal identity, national identity, cultural practices, and spiritual identity are totally intertwined. To be interested in issues of faith is to be interested in them as persons.

I asked Moussa about his family and he reciprocated. After Moussa went back to work, Bobby commented, "This is the first time in my life that I've ever talked with a Muslim."

My longtime friend Larry Anzivino has been encouraging a global mindset in others for many years. He offered these shallow-end starters for families desiring to build a John 3:16 "love the world" home environment:

- Use the internet to learn about life in a foreign culture. Help children see that people actually live in the countries they see on the map.

- Connect the global world to daily life at home. Talk about athletes from other nations, look for country-specific stickers on bananas, explain foreign phrases in our vocabulary.

- Host an international student or a friend from another culture for dinner. Help children know people of different cultures and ethnicities, skin color, and language.

- Attend cultural events in other ethnic neighborhoods to develop an appreciation for other traditions.

- Support an international project or a child overseas as a family.[2]

When we start going global with even these small strokes, it opens a new world of growth for us and our families.

INTO THE DEEPER WATER—
MAYBE UP TO A FOURTH OF A MILE

After we grow accustomed to the international outreach we can have from our home base, we can venture out a little farther. Now the risks, sacrifice, and investments take on greater commitments.

Language learning. It's time-consuming, sometimes humiliating, and more challenging the older we get, but it equips us to communicate more with bilingual neighbors as well as people outside our communities. And it is a great asset for young people. Young adults who enter the world after university with a fluency in languages like Spanish or Chinese or Arabic will be more equipped for the future. Language learning is a definite commitment to expand our cultural diversity in the internationalized world in which we live.

English teaching or tutoring. How about becoming a teacher or tutor in a local ESL class? It provides lots of opportunities to learn, give, and build relationships with people. And in the case of foreign students or immigrants and refugees, it often provides a chance to build a friendship with people from countries where they may not have ever heard the message of John 3:16.

Cross an ethnic divide intentionally. If God's love is for "the world" we can reflect his heart by venturing out of our own communities. At our home church (a predominantly white, middle-class, suburban church), the deep end includes service ventures into the city or shared worship with other ethnic-specific churches.

John Perkins, a civil rights leader and founder of the Christian Community Development Association, exhorts Christians against the "dangers of a homogeneous fellowship." He encourages everyone to have Christian brothers and sisters from many racial and ethnic backgrounds. He observes that "belonging to a group whose members are like oneself requires no faith. . . . Reconciling bigots is a far greater sign of the supernatural than is speaking in tongues."[3]

Think globally but act locally. Going global might not involve international travel. Carol takes meals weekly to a homeless shelter as an expression of God's love. Phil and Pat lead a youth group of Rohingya refugee children at a nearby church. Steve offers his construction services to inner-city ministries. Les and Jan and their family sacrifice their traditional Thanksgiving celebration and join a homeless ministry by serving the street people of a major city.

See the people others might avoid. Let us never forget the physically or mentally challenged groups that might be geographically near us but outside of our cultural or social orbit. They have a subculture of their own that needs to be penetrated with the love of Christ. And yet, the risks we take are real; we will feel awkward at first to work with the chronically ill, hearing-impaired, blind, or mentally ill.

Going deeper takes us into the world where people from other cultures and ethnic groups live so that we might, in a small way, identify with them and their worlds. Following the example of Jesus (John 1:14), involvement sends us out to be a physical expression (*incarnate*) his love.

READY TO SWIM A MILE?

Many years ago, a travel agency near Harvard University advertised travel with three words: Please . . . Go Away. I've never forgotten the slogan because when I read of God's love for the world and I recite Jesus' command to make disciples of all nations (Matthew 28:18-20), I hear him saying, in effect, "Please . . . Go Away."

The first white missionary, Adoniram Judson, was sent from the shores of North America in 1812, a time in which global travel for the average person was out of the question. It took him three months to sail from the East Coast of the United States to India.[4] Today, however, we can travel from New York City directly to India in about fifteen hours.

Traveling into other countries and experiencing other cultures is open to us as never before. With appropriate planning and saving, all of us can venture out to have our worldviews expanded by travel. The "God so loved the world" of John 3:16 will move from words on the page to people with names, needs, cultures, and languages.

Will expands his view of the world God loves by extending his international business trips. His consultant position has him overseas four times per year—often in countries that oppress Christianity. He extends his trips over weekends and uses his free time to visit national churches, encourage Christian workers, and learn about the stresses of crosscultural adaptation. His growth comes with a risk because it means leaving the security of Americanized compounds or conference centers and getting out on the streets of Beijing, Bogota, or Delhi. But by making advance contact with believers who live there, he is escorted by people who know the language and culture.

Hank is a single man who spends his vacation time on crosscultural trips. He leads church-based service teams or simply travels with some of the "adventure travel" groups to grow in his world vision. These trips have resulted in Hank's service on the outreach team at his church and increased financial commitments to the support of international projects.

Crosscultural service teams must never become some sort of affluent voyeurism, what are sometimes critiqued as "Poor Tours." Instead, they should offer involvement. Get dusty. Stay for two weeks with a local family in another culture. Learn what the tourists never learn.

The higher risks of such travel are worth it because they offer growth and service opportunities that allow us to live alongside of brothers and sisters from every tribe, tongue, and nation, giving us a "preview of heaven" as we get a glimpse of the multicultural worship services described in Revelation 5:9 and 7:9.

LIVE SENT

Twenty-five years ago, when more of our North American culture had a modest amount of biblical literacy, it was quite common to see a person at an athletic event holding a poster that said "John 3:16" or even "JN 3:16." The person might position themselves behind the catcher in a baseball game, the goal posts in a football game, the basket in a basketball game, or the goals in a hockey or soccer game. The positioning was both for the fans in the stadium and for the TV cameras broadcasting the game. When the pitcher pitched, the kicker attempted a field goal, the player shot free throws, or the other team had a shot on net, the sign would come up. I'm sure these "evangelists" had good intentions, but I've never encountered anyone who had a moment of spiritual hunger provoked by a glance at a Bible verse reference behind the backboard as his favorite basketball player shot free throws.

The concept of posting the reference in front of us Christians to remind us that we are called by God to live out his invitation of love and belief might have some validity. Maybe the church ushers should hold up John 3:16 posters as we leave church and enter the work week! Or maybe the church parking lot attendant could stand at the exit with John 3:16 placards.

Probably a better idea is to find a way to keep the verse in front of us personally: a sticky note on the refrigerator, an onscreen note with all or part of the verse spelled out, or a note on the dashboard as we linger in traffic with people who are *not* experiencing love at that moment. The goal is to live out John 3:16 in our context, at our jobs, in our schools, or in our communities, and we need to find a way to remind ourselves.

At the Urbana 03 student missions conference, Pastor John Teter delivered a powerful message challenging us all to live daily as witnesses for Jesus Christ. A phrase he used has stuck with me as a short-form reminder of living the invitation of John 3:16 every day. At the end of his time, he simply paused and offered these words: "Live sent."

Maybe we should forego the posters and placards and simply put a sign over our door as we exit into the community, our jobs, our schools, the world: "Live sent." Or maybe we should tattoo these words on our hands or our hearts: "Live sent." Why?

For God so loved the world that he gave his one and only Son, that whoever believes in him shall not perish but have eternal life.

EPILOGUE

ALWAYS ON MISSION

I boarded the plane for a cross-country flight, secretly hoping that the seat next to me would be empty. A stimulating conference had left me tired and ready for some downtime. I looked forward to reading, watching a movie, or taking a snooze. I sat down in seat 12A and thanked God that 12B was empty . . . until Jim joined me.[1]

We exchanged cordial greetings and I returned to my reading. Within minutes Jim let it be known that he wanted to talk. My mind flashed to all the reasons why I didn't want to get into a long, cross-country conversation. I was tired. Not at my best. Who is Jim? Will we end up just talking about drivel? How do I get out of this conversation?

A phrase from the book *Divine Appointments* came to mind: "24-7 availability," which means being always available and willing to be a witness for Christ twenty-four hours a day, seven days a week.[2] I prayed, "Lord, strengthen me now to listen to Jim, to draw him out, to be your witness."

When Paul exhorted Timothy to be prepared always to "preach the word; be prepared in season and out of season," (2 Timothy 4:2) he was calling Timothy (and us!) to 24-7 availability, no matter the circumstances. When Paul wrote these words, he was facing much greater challenges than feeling tired when facing a chatty co-traveler on a cross-country flight.

Paul wrote these words from prison facing imminent death. He was in perhaps the toughest season of his life and ministry. He was lonely, he had been deserted by coworkers, and he was physically suffering (2 Timothy 4:9, 10, 13, 14, 16). But he practiced what he preached: church tradition records the names of multiple prisoners and prison guards that Paul led to faith in Christ before he was executed. Scholars believe that Paul and Peter both spent their last days before execution in the Mamertine prison in Rome. It's likely that Paul wrote 2 Timothy from this dimly lit cell. If you go there today (it's an historical attraction), you'll see a plaque with dozens of names of people who were led to Christ by Paul and Peter while they were prisoners.

How can we cultivate this "in season and out of season" attitude so that we are always on our 3:16 mission as witnesses to the hope that we have in Jesus? Here are a few suggestions.

OPEN YOUR EYES

When Jesus encounters a crowd, he sees them as "harassed and helpless, like sheep without a shepherd"

(Matthew 9:36). In a similar encounter, the disciples ask Jesus to send the people away (Matthew 14:14-15). The difference is vision: Jesus saw the people through eyes of compassion. The disciples saw them as an inconvenience. We need to change the way we look at people.

My attitude toward Jim on the airplane—or my neighbors, coworkers, or the international fellow who serves me at the supermarket—changes when I ask God to help me see them with eyes of compassion. That man sitting next to me is an eternal soul with an eternal destiny (Ecclesiastes 3:11; Hebrews 9:27). Those people I encounter through the week are loved by God (John 3:16; Romans 5:8), but they might not know it. When I see others through the eyes of Jesus, I realize that it's my privilege to be God's witness to his 3:16 love.

OPEN YOUR SCHEDULE

In a context similar to Paul writing to Timothy, Peter wrote to suffering, persecuted Christians urging them always to be prepared (in spite of their circumstances) to give a response to others—explaining the "reason for the hope that you have" (1 Peter 3:15).

When I boarded that plane, I had my own agenda, but God's agenda for me included Jim. I turned my attention toward him, and he talked. Most people are deeply attracted to someone who will *listen* to them! Being available means being willing to focus my attention on the person or people God has put right in front of me.

A study of Philip provides a great picture of the open-scheduled available witness (Acts 8). Wherever he went, he looked for opportunities to serve, preach, and impact others for Jesus' sake. As a deacon, he served the immediate needs before him (Acts 6:1-7). As an everyday witness, he preached to Samaritans (Acts 8:4); launched into an unexpected encounter with an exotic foreigner, the Ethiopian eunuch (Acts 8:27); and resumed preaching when he found himself in Azotus (Acts 8:40). Philip exemplifies a believer in search of divine appointments. Rather than looking at interruptions and unexpected human encounters as inconveniences, he responded to them as opportunities sovereignly created by God.

In a day and age when time may be our most valued resource, opening our schedules to others can be tough. For many of us, "in season and out of season" might be translated "when it's convenient and when it's not; when it fits our schedules and when it interrupts our plans." Making time to listen to a coworker, an aged neighbor, or an interrupting child might be the availability challenge we face.

OPEN THE NEWS

Look for "hooks"—what news items are people already interested in that you can then connect to the gospel? One of the best biblical examples of this is Paul in Acts 17. He walked around and observed the spiritual context of Athens, and he used the spiritual interests of the Athenians as a bridge to introducing them to Jesus.

In the past year, I've gotten into conversations with people around a host of topics, including the economy, events in the Middle East, and major league baseball. But as one who desires availability as a witness, I'm looking and praying for ways to direct these conversations to a spiritual discussion.

Interactions on the economy has led to questions like, "What are we trusting as we face the future?" Events in the Middle East have led to discussions on the difference of Christian faith from other religions. Even banter around baseball—and the sports slogan "I live for this"—has led to the question, "What are we living for?"

OPEN YOUR PRAYERS

For forty years, my wife set the tone for "in season" and "out of season" witness by arriving early to the medical laboratory where she worked and praying for the people who worked there, following the 1 Thessalonians 5:17 mandate to "pray continually." A high school student I know does the same thing on Monday mornings by taking a prayer walk through the corridors of the school. At attitude of prayer gives us the anticipation that God is going to work.

J. Christy Wilson, my professor and a former missionary in Afghanistan, often expressed his love for people in the Muslim faith. To this day I follow his exhortation to pray for people from other faiths that we see in our cities, at our schools, or in the airport. He told me, "When you see someone whose attire or symbols tell you they are from another world religion, breathe a prayer for them because you might be praying for someone who has never been prayed for before in Jesus' name." God works through our prayers to prepare us, but he also uses prayer to prepare those who will receive the gospel.

OPEN YOUR HANDS

For many of us, our witness is most visible to our neighbors. Practical service is a bridge to the gospel in almost any culture—a way to demonstrate our faith by our deeds, as stated in James 2:18. Some might serve their neighbors by helping a newly arrived person get their documentation in order. Others might start an ESL program. Others can simply provide hospitality, help in the yard, run an errand, or help with a house project. People might respond to the actions of our hands and feet long before they listen to our words.

Which brings me back to my cross-country seatmate, Jim. Though my emotions were definitely in the out-of-season mode, I started asking questions. I discovered that Jim is a professional gourmet chef, so we talked about some of the reality TV shows depicting life in the kitchen for gourmet chefs. This led to discussing some of the tensions in Jim's life. This led to conversation about family. And this led to conversation about faith, prayer, church, and life direction.

We talked for more than three hours. When we went our separate ways, Jim left thinking of the questions I had raised and the invitation I had given him to begin a new relationship with Jesus. I left praying for Jim, that our conversation might be a seed of the gospel planted in his life—that he would know that the pursuing God so loves him and sent Jesus to bring him eternal life.

We are always on mission. May God accomplish his mission 3:16 through us.

NOTES

INTRODUCTION

[1]Elisabeth Elliot, *Discipline: The Glad Surrender* (Grand Rapids, MI: Baker Books, 2006), 33. I have modified her quotation from "man" to "human beings" and "men" to "men and women."

[2]"Elevator pitch," Wikipedia.org, https://en.wikipedia.org /wiki/Elevator_pitch.

[3]William Barclay, *The Gospel of John, Vol. 1*, rev. ed., The Daily Study Bible Series (Philadelphia: The Westminster Press, 1975), 137-38.

[4]Anne Graham Lotz, CeCe Winans, Frank S. Page, and Max Lucado quoted in Max Lucado, *3:16: The Numbers of Hope* (Nashville: Thomas Nelson, 2007), i-iii, 3, 7.

[5]G. J. Wenham, J. A. Motyer, D. A. Carson, and R. T. France, eds., *The New Bible Commentary,* rev. ed. (Downers Grove, IL: InterVarsity Press, 1987), 937.

1. ENTERING INTO JOHN 3

[1]See *The Life with God Bible* (NRSV) with contributors Richard J. Foster, Dallas Willard, Walter Brueggemann, and Eugene H. Peterson (New York: HarperOne, 2005), 160.

[2]D. L. Moody, *Notes from My Bible* (New York: Fleming H. Revell Company, 1895), 135.

[3]"Karl Barth, Courageous Theologian," Christian History, *Christianity Today*, www.christianitytoday.com/history/people /theologians/karl-barth.html, accessed October 10, 2019.

[4]"Life" entry, *Dictionary of Jesus and the Gospels*, Joel B. Green, ed. (Downers Grove, IL: InterVarsity Press, 2013), 469-70.

[5]W. E. Vine, "Only Begotten" entry, *Vine's Complete Expository Dictionary of Old and New Testament Words* (Nashville: Thomas Nelson, 1996), 140.

[6]This summary also appears in Paul Borthwick, *Western Christians in Global Mission: What's the Role of the North American Church?* (Downers Grove, IL: InterVarsity Press, 2012), 116-17.

2. "FOR GOD"

[1]Bob Jacks and Matthew R. Jacks, *Divine Appointments* (Colorado Springs, CO: NavPress, 2002), chap. 2.

[2]Scott W. Sunquist, *Why Church? A Basic Introduction* (Downers Grove, IL: IVP Academic, 2019), 139, 140, 141, 154.

[3]Paul Borthwick, *Western Christians in Global Mission: What's the Role of the North American Church?* (Downers Grove, IL: InterVarsity Press, 2012), 42-43.

[4]William Barclay, *The Letters to the Corinthians*, rev. ed., The Daily Study Bible Series (Louisville, KY: Westminster John Knox, 1975), 210.

[5]Emmanuel Katongole and Chris Rice, *Reconciling All Things: A Christian Vision for Justice, Peace and Healing* (Downers Grove, IL: InterVarsity Press, 2008), 51-52.

3. "SO LOVED"

[1]"A Good News Name," *Evangelicals* magazine, Winter 2017/2018, 6, www.nae.net/evangelicals-winter-2017-18.

[2]Brother Andrew, "I Sincerely Love All Muslims," Open Doors, https://opendoorsyouth.org/article/i-sincerely-love-all-muslims.

[3]Simi Chakrabarti, "Widow of Murdered Missionary Chooses to Stay in India," *The World Today*, September 8, 2003, www.abc.net.au/worldtoday/content/2003/s941513.htm.

[4]This story was relayed to me during a 2006 visit to Sri Lanka by members of a church-planting movement called Kithu Sevana, which concentrates on work in southern Sri Lanka. They were deeply involved in tsunami relief.

[5]Nairy Ohanian, *Now, Can You Trust Me? Stories of Faith and Adventure in Armenia* (n.p.: Ohanian Publishing, 2007).

[6]Jayme Poisson, "Afghanistan: 'We Don't Hold Hate in Our Hearts,'" *The Star*, Oct. 21, 2011, www.thestar.com/news/insight/2011/10/21/afghanistan_we_dont_hold_hate_in_our_hearts.html.

4. "THE WORLD"

[1]D. L. Moody, *Notes from My Bible* (New York: Fleming H. Revell Company, 1895), 136.

[2]See the Joshua Project (https://joshuaproject.net) for a variety of ways to connect with, learn about, and pray for the unreached and unengaged people groups of the world.

[3]This story also appears in Paul Borthwick, *Great Commission, Great Compassion* (Downers Grove, IL: InterVarsity Press, 2015), 171.

[4]Todd Johnson, *Religious Demography and Global Christian Education*, presented to the trustees of Wheaton College, IL, February 10, 2012.

[5]Johnson, *Religious Demography*, citing Ian Goldin, Geoffrey Cameron, and Meera Balarajan, *Exceptional People: How Migration Shaped our World and Will Define Our Future* (Princeton, NJ: Princeton University Press, 2011).

[6]See Mark Labberton, ed., *Still Evangelical? Insiders Reconsider Political, Social, and Theological Meaning* (Downers Grove, IL: InterVarsity Press, 2018).

5. "THAT HE GAVE"

[1]Read more about this historic conference at www.lausanne.org/gatherings/congress/cape-town-2010-3.

[2]See www.elam.com for more about Elam ministries.

[3]Joel Osteen, *Your Best Life Now: 7 Steps to Living at Your Full Potential* (New York: FaithWords, 2014).

[4]C. T. Studd, quoted in Paul Borthwick, *Missions: God's Heart for the World* (Downers Grove, IL: InterVarsity Press, 2000), 67.

[5]Paul Borthwick and Dave Ripper, *The Fellowship of the Suffering* (Downers Grove, IL: InterVarsity Press, 2018), 176.

[6]This section is slightly adapted from Paul Borthwick, "Get Out of Your Bubble," Paulborthwick.com blog, August 15, 2018, www.paulborthwick.com/get-out-of-your-bubble/. Used courtesy of Paul Borthwick.

[7]John Ortberg, *If You Want to Walk on Water, You've Got to Get Out of the Boat* (Grand Rapids, MI: Zondervan, 2001).

[8]John Henry Jowett, quoted in Gary Inrig, *A Call to Excellence* (Wheaton, IL: Victor Books, 1985), 51.

6. "HIS ONE AND ONLY SON"

[1]Source unknown. It's attributed to E. Stanley Jones because of his creation of and involvement in these Round Table discussions and because of his belief in the uniqueness of Jesus Christ.

[2]Max Lucado, *3:16: The Numbers of Hope* (Nashville: Thomas Nelson, 2007), 45.

[3]Robert Boyd Munger, *My Heart—Christ's Home* (Downers Grove, IL: InterVarsity Press, 1954).

[4]Robertson McQuilkin, *The Great Omission* (Grand Rapids, MI: Baker Books, 1984), 50-51.

7. "THAT WHOEVER BELIEVES IN HIM"

[1]Max Lucado, *3:16: The Numbers of Hope* (Nashville: Thomas Nelson, 2007), 66.

[2]I highly recommend Winfried Corduan, *Neighboring Faiths*, second ed. (Downers Grove, IL: InterVarsity Press, 2012). It not only explains world religions and worldviews but also adds "So you meet a person of [this faith]" at the close of every chapter so that the reader has concrete next steps on how to foster dialogue.

8. "SHALL NOT PERISH"

[1]The first part of this story appeared in my book *Six Dangerous Questions* (Downers Grove, IL: InterVarsity Press, 1996), 68-69. In that book, we didn't identify Rocco specifically because 1) he was still alive, and 2) we didn't know the end of the story yet.

[2]I have wrestled with these questions for a very long time. Anyone who reads John 3:16-18 and wants to honor the integrity of the "shall not perish" phrase will do the same. For my more extensive examination of these and other questions, check out my book *Six Dangerous Questions* (Downers Grove, IL: InterVarsity Press, 1996), specifically the chapter "Do I Believe in Hell?" Other helpful resources

are Ajith Fernando, *Crucial Questions About Hell* (East-bourne, UK: Kingsway, 1991); Edward William Fudge and Robert A. Peterson, *Two Views of Hell: A Biblical and Theological Dialogue* (Downers Grove, IL: InterVarsity Press, 2000); and Stanley N. Gundry, Dennis L. Okholm, Timothy R. Phillips, eds., *Four Views on Salvation in a Pluralistic World* (Grand Rapids, MI: Zondervan, 1996).

[3]Timothy C. Tennent, *Christianity at the Religious Roundtable* (Grand Rapids, MI: Baker Academic, 2002), 17.

[4]Tennent, *Christianity at the Religious Roundtable*, 26.

[5]Carl G. Vaught, *Access to God in Augustine's Confessions, Books X-XIII* (Albany, NY: State University of New York, 2005), 33.

[6]Al Tizon, *Whole & Reconciled: Gospel, Church, and Mission in a Fractured World* (Grand Rapids, MI: Baker Books, 2018), 65-66.

[7]Tizon, *Whole & Reconciled*, 66.

[8]Robert Robinson, "Come, Thou Fount of Every Blessing," 1758.

9. "BUT HAVE ETERNAL LIFE"

[1]Eugene Peterson, *A Long Obedience in the Same Direction: Discipleship in an Instant Society*, commemorative ed. (Downers Grove, IL: InterVarsity Press, 2019).

[2]Paul Tournier, *The Adventure of Living* (New York: Harper and Row, 1963).

[3]*The Best Exotic Marigold Hotel*, directed by John Madden (London: Blueprint Pictures, 2011).

10. THE CHALLENGE

[1]This section is adapted from Paul Borthwick, *How to Be a World-Class Christian* (Downers Grove, IL: InterVarsity Press, 2009), 142-49.

[2]Personal communication, used courtesy of Larry Anzivino.

[3]John Perkins speaking at the mission conference of Grace Chapel in Lexington, MA, on October 17, 1982.

[4]The Editors of Encyclopaedia Britannica, "Adoniram Judson, American Missionary," *Encyclopaedia Britannica*, www.britannica.com/biography/Adoniram-Judson.

EPILOGUE

[1]This is updated and revised from Paul Borthwick, "Everyday Witness," *Decision Magazine*, November 30, 2011, https://decisionmagazine.com/everyday-witness. Used courtesy of Paul Borthwick.

[2]Bob Jacks and Matthew R. Jacks, *Divine Appointments* (Colorado Springs, CO: NavPress, 2002), 23.

ALSO BY PAUL BORTHWICK

6 Dangerous Questions to Transform Your View of the World
978-0-8308-1685-9

The Fellowship of Suffering
With coauthor Dave Ripper
978-0-8308-4530-9

Great Commission, Great Compassion
978-0-8308-4437-1

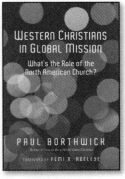

Western Christians in Global Mission
978-0-8308-3780-9

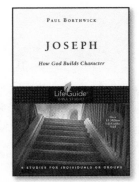

Joseph: How God Builds Character
(LifeGuide Bible Studies)
978-0-8308-3049-7

Missions: God's Heart for the World
(LifeGuide Bible Studies)
978-0-8308-3090-9

To learn more about
Development Associates International,
go to daintl.org.

To read blogs by Paul,
see his schedule, or contact him,
go to paulborthwick.com.